# AN ANARCHIST'S STORY

# An Anarchist's Story

## The Life of Ethel Macdonald

CHRIS DOLAN

BIRLINN

For Antonio González, James Maley, Steve Fullarton, Antonia Fantanillas,
every *brigadista*, for actually fighting the fight, keeping the faith.
*Adelante!* is the cry around the hillside.

First published in 2009 by
Birlinn Limited
West Newington House
10 Newington Road
Edinburgh
EH9 1QS

*www.birlinn.co.uk*

ISBN: 978 1 84158 685 4

British Library Cataloguing-in-Publication Data
A catalogue record for this book is available from the British Library

Designed and typeset by Edderston Book Design
Printed and bound by CPI Cox & Wyman, Reading

Governments will never save the people. They exist to exploit and destroy the people. There is but one force that can save the people – and that is the people themselves.

*Ethel Macdonald*

# Contents

# List of Illustrations

Andrew and Daisy Macdonald at Calder Road, Bellshill, 1940s.

Camelia Ethel's birth certificate.

Ethel, in her late teens.

Young Guy Aldred.

Smoke rises over Barcelona after air raids by General Franco's Nationalist forces, March 1936.

A militiawoman holding high ground on the Aragon Front against the rebels.

Dolores Ibarruri, 'La Pasionaria'.

Ministry of Propaganda poster (1936/7) to galvanize international support for the Republic.

CNT poster, produced in conjunction with the UGT, during the early months of the war.

Ministry of Propaganda, 1936. The artist, Juan Antonio Morales, depicts the elements of Nationalist support.

Juan Miró's 1937 poster was used to rouse support in France.

Mujeres Libres poster: 'Your family is everyone who fights for Liberty!'

Anti-prostitution poster: 'There is a new life for you, offering dignified work and a human existence'.

'The radio receiver is the mouthpiece of culture in the home of the worker! Respect it! Everyone should have one'.

Announcement giving times of Ethel's talks from Spain.

Graphic Republican poster.

Ethel on her lecture tour after her return from Spain.

Guernica, after the Condor Legion bombing, April 1937.

Ethel visiting home, perhaps for the last time.

Bessie (Elizabeth), Freddie's mother and Ethel's younger sister in her ATS uniform at the start of the Second World War.

'Wee' Freddie, with his dad, Freddie, and mother, Ethel's sister, Bessie.

# *Author's Note*

Despite years of interest in the Spanish Civil War, I had never come across the name Ethel Macdonald. I finally did so through a series of accidents.

I was preparing a script for a film about another wrongly forgotten Scottish woman, Jane Haining – a Church of Scotland governess in Budapest who was arrested by the Nazis in 1944 and sent to Auschwitz, where she died for protecting the children in her care. Alison Murphy, the film's producer, happened upon the Ethel Macdonald Collection in Glasgow's Mitchell Library and being of a doggedly inquiring disposition soon 'discovered' a story that immediately replaced the film we had been working on.

In the collection Alison found a pamphlet entitled 'Ethel Macdonald: Glasgow Woman Anarchist' by Rhona Hodgart, published in 2003. This was the only existing study that told the key facts of Ethel's life. Rhona had uncovered new information, and interviewed John Taylor Caldwell, Ethel's flatmate, comrade and sometime lover. Alison interviewed John again in 2006, sadly just before he died, while we were making *An Anarchist's Story* for Pelicula Films, directed by Mark Littlewood.

This book takes Rhona's work and Alison's research for the film as its starting point. In 2008, I got in touch with Freddie Turrell, Ethel's nephew. He had seen the film on television and had made contact with the BBC. Freddie knew, and remembers, his Auntie Ethel. He filled in many of the blanks, telling me about events and dramas in Ethel's personal life that completely change our understanding of her. His relationship with her, the stories he garnered from Ethel's brothers and sisters, and from her own mother – still alive when Freddie was young – give us a fuller picture of a woman caught up in historic international events.

More information about the situation Ethel walked into – quite literally – in November 1936 comes from several experts. I spent several hours with Noam Chomsky in his study at the Massachusetts Institute of Technology. As well as being Professor Emeritus of Linguistics at MIT, Noam Chomsky is an anarchist with a keen interest in and deep knowledge of European politics of the 1930s. I talked throughout the writing of this book with Professor Mike Gonzalez of Glasgow University – as Rhona Hodgart's tutor, it was he who first suggested that she look into the history of a neglected anarchist from Motherwell. Mike puts Ethel's activities into perspective and helps explain the complex political geography of Spain at the beginning of the Civil War. Mike's connection is more than academic – his father fought with the Republic and had to flee to London from Franco's vengeful victory. Willy Maley, Professor of Renaissance Studies, is not only a colleague of Mike's at Glasgow University, but also shares a deep personal connection with the battle for Spain. His father, James Maley, was a *brigadista*, a Scottish volunteer who went to Spain to fight the fascists. James died in April 2007 (his friend Steve Fullarton died in February 2008, the last of the Scottish *brigadistas*). He was a lifelong communist but, as he and his son Willy make clear, no sectarian. The enemy was the fascist threat in Spain. Willy has been kind enough to give a communist perspective on the biography of an anti-communist.

Two years ago, Mark Littlewood and I went to Dreux, a small town northwest of Paris, to interview an astonishing woman. Antonia Fontanillas is now in her late eighties but is increasingly recognised as an eloquent witness to the Spanish Revolution. Antonia lived and worked through the heady days of 1936–7 in her home city, Barcelona. The two young women did not know one another personally, but Antonia's testimony here brings Ethel's Barcelona to life.

I am indebted to all these people and more, including Professor Maria Dolors Genovés Morales for her contribution to the film and this book, and John Taylor Caldwell, who is the only contemporary source other than Freddie Turrell who knew Ethel personally. *Come Dungeons Dark*, and other writings of Caldwell's are the closest first-hand sources we have. John Couzin's biographical essay is one of the few overviews to date, along with Rhona Hodgart's work and the obituary Aldred wrote on Ethel's death. Noam Chomsky's general writing on history and politics has been a useful comparison to Eric Hobsbawm's on the same events. Radical journals such as *Revolutionary History* and publications by the Clydeside Press have all helped me build a picture of Ethel Macdonald. While I was writing my book, Daniel Gray was working on his excellent *Homage to Caledonia; Scotland and the Spanish Civil War*. Daniel's research turned up several intriguing eleventh-hour revelations.

Where the facts desert us – because she herself saw them

as unworthy of being recorded, or because few people felt that the efforts of a Glasgow radical merited documenting – we try and find her in what we do know about her world: Scotland, Spain, the ideas and ideals of her time, the radical history of Glasgow, and the bloody events in Barcelona in 1936 and 1937.

Best of all, exactly a century after her birth, we still have the words of Ethel herself. Not everything she wrote about her time in Spain has been found, or saved, but there is enough to get to know something of a woman our history has disgracefully stifled. A restless, justice-seeking spirit, a woman of her time, with a message that will make as much sense, and provoke as much contention and discussion, today.

# Introduction

In 1936, war was sweeping over Spain, and although Barcelona was preparing for battle, there was an air of optimism and exhilaration. The city was in the throes of the most profound revolution of the twentieth century. Workers ran businesses by committee; the police force had been abolished; 2,000 years of sexual politics had been overturned. Anarchism – not anarchy – for the only time in its history was the official state system.

Newly arrived in the city, Ethel Macdonald, a working-class girl from Motherwell, walked down Las Ramblas one November morning with a notebook in her hand. She knew no shorthand and could barely type, but her early observations of the city would form the first of many dispatches to grow in import and drama over the next ten months.

> Civilian soldiers dressed in dungarees and little red and black 'Glengarry' bonnets, smoking endless cigarettes, strolled casually in Las Ramblas and the Via Durruti, or chatted to the girl soldiers in the Plaza Catalunya. We had difficulty deciding which were young men and which were girls. They were dressed exactly alike, but as we drew nearer we saw that all the girls had beautifully 'permed' hair and were strikingly made up.

The first things Ethel would have sought out were the

various crucial military centres in the city. In the Via Laietana (renamed then Via Durruti after the anarchist leader) the telephone exchange and Chamber of Commerce were held by the Anarchist National Confederation of Labour. The socialists and communists were uptown in the Paseo de Gracia. In between were the headquarters of the Workers' Party of Marxist Unification, Trotskyists to whom George Orwell was attached, and, of course, the Generalitat, the seat of Catalonia's Republican government. All these organisations fought together against the Nationalist military which, in November 1936, was just over 200 miles away at Zaragoza. There were tensions between them, however, which Ethel, although only just arrived, knew all about. Turning back to Las Ramblas, she would look up at the red-and-black anarchist banners and the Catalan flags flying from most buildings and notice that there were very few hammers and sickles.

Ethel Macdonald was to become, for a few short months, one of the world's most famous voices. She was perhaps the first example of an 'embedded reporter', sending dispatches and broadcasts back from the Spanish anarchist camp. But she made no pretence of impartiality or balance of opinion. Ethel had been a socialist for many years, but had little faith in parliaments – and none in authoritarian communism – delivering anything for working people. She believed passionately in justice; she dreamed and worked for a fairer, more genuinely democratic world. She was utterly committed to anarchism and revolution. But these ideals were not the comic-book clichés that their enemies even today like to portray. Ethel Macdonald's anarchism was in search of peace, reason and liberty.

Surely a working-class girl, forged in the poverty and workshops of industrial western Scotland, and born on the eve of the Russian Revolution, would have become, like her family and many of her friends, a socialist, a communist? Anarchism was hardly the norm in Motherwell in the early part of last century. Or perhaps it was a greater force than we care to remember.

The term Scottish anarchist is restrictive; Ethel Macdonald saw herself also as a radical, a socialist, a feminist. What mattered was working for a decent, free society. In that aim, she takes her place in a long Scottish tradition. From the Celtic Church, through the Reformation, the Enlightenment, the Red Clydesiders and the General Strike, Scotland has played its part in the struggle for egalitarianism and freedom.

Mystery surrounds Ethel Macdonald, from her birth certificate to the last days of her life. Working-class people do not leave much evidence behind them. History belongs to the rich and the powerful: they write themselves in, and airbrush out the irksome hoi polloi. Every once in a while a single voice makes itself heard. History belongs, too, of course, to the victors. Anarchism's most glorious period was not to last. Thus the lives and hopes of an entire generation, in Madrid and Valencia and across Spain, but most importantly, for us, in Catalonia, are lost. The Spanish fascists, as you would expect, had nothing good – or often even true – to say about them. Forty years of Franco's destructive, mean-spirited and reactionary government all but wiped out the memory of the Spanish Revolution. The communists, too, who were soon to play a vital part in the ending of that revolution, would prefer that we forget all about the anarchists and their extraordinary achievements.

Of Ethel's time in Spain we know almost everything. She left behind her – hidden and until recently forgotten in Glasgow's Mitchell Library – articles and letters, and scripts of her radio broadcasts from Barcelona. Ten months after her hopeful arrival in Spain, the messenger became the story. So we have records of speeches made in the House of Commons, negotiations made on her behalf and newspaper appeals to find the Bellshill Anarchist.

We know, too, about her relentless work for peace and social justice after her return from Spain until her tragic early death. About her private and personal life, however, Ethel herself has kept us in the dark.

Like many dedicated people, her focus was singular. Her work in defending the rights of the poor, fighting the corner of the unrepresented against government and employers, was all-consuming. What happened behind closed doors, in her own personal life, she did not so much conceal as consider irrelevant. The vast majority of her time and energy was dedicated to the cause she lived for, and there are periods of her life about which Ethel didn't inform her family or even her comrades and friends, and left no record. Nonetheless, there are some clues which can help us build a fuller picture of Ethel Macdonald. We know a lot about the town of her birth, the Glasgow that became her home, the time she grew up in, the hardships, the politics and the vibrancy of the people who nurtured her growing commitment that led, eventually, to her own courageous activities in Spain. There are also the mentions her lifelong friend John Taylor Caldwell made in books, interviews and articles, as well as the memories of her younger sister, Carrie. Carrie died in 2008, at 88. Until then, she shared her memories with Freddie Turrell, her nephew. Freddie's own memories and anecdotes have contributed enormously to this book.

∽

In July 1937 newspaper headlines announced that Ethel Macdonald had been arrested and jailed in Spain and would soon be tried. In an article smuggled out of Barcelona she described the scene of her arrest:

> One night at about 1 o'clock there was a thunderous knocking at the door. Assault Guards marched in and, without a word of explanation, ransacked every corner and every cupboard . . . They took me the police station, and left me there all night. They wanted me to sign some document, but I refused.
>
> The next morning I was moved to the Hotel Falcon – which had become a prison for anarchist soldiers. They took me in a motor-lorry that for all the world was like the tumbrel of the French Revolution.

When Ethel then fell silent she became the focus of an international search and intergovernmental negotiations. Through further smuggled articles she described how she escaped, but that she could not leave Spain for fear of being arrested again. Beyond Barcelona, Ethel was dubbed 'the Scots Scarlet Pimpernel' and 'the Stormy Petrel'. Editors and readers demanded action, fearing the worst when there was no word from her. Ethel had been imprisoned by her erstwhile comrades in the Republican government – the

Republic she had gone to Spain to help, whose story she was determined to tell to the wider world. What happened to her, and how she finally won through, is not just the story of one woman's struggle, but a fascinating insight into a time and a revolution that for many years has been almost wiped from public memory. Ethel's experiences, as she herself was always at pains to point out, were much bigger than herself.

She was part of a generation of dedicated people – mainly men – who left their families, jobs and security to fight for an ideal in a distant country. Ethel was different not just for being female. Her hopes for Spain were much more radical than those of the Republican government or the socialist- and communist-backed militias. Some might argue today, as they did then, that those hopes were *too* radical, unrealistic. But she was hardly alone – the vast majority of the Catalan people not only shared her vision but had been carefully making it a reality for two years before Ethel's arrival and during her first months in Barcelona. The men who came from Scotland, England, Ireland, Germany, Italy and almost every conceivable part of Europe and the New World fought alongside the Spanish people to halt the rise of fascism. The question was, and remains to this day, to replace it with what? Many international *brigadistas* were inspired by the communist ideal, others had no notion that there were alternatives until they got there. What was the point, Ethel and the Catalan people asked, in fighting one tyranny only to replace it with another?

We can use Ethel Macdonald's story to ponder both positions. Was it better to be less radical and simply win the war against the extreme right's advance through Spain? Were the anarchists, as the Republican government and their allies claimed, risking the loss of a crucial battle? Or was it the Republic's attack on their allies, creating a battle within a battle, that helped Franco claim victory?

Ethel herself had a lot to say on the question. Finally out of Spain, but with no hope of returning to help in the war, she spoke to crowds in France, Holland, London and, on her return home, Glasgow. These speeches are a record of a fundamental ideal that refuses to die: the notion of a truly democratic and just society, free of coercion and oppression.

Ethel's story is also, of course, one of defeat – a personal loss and, more importantly, a national loss in Catalonia and Spain generally. Fascism won out, and perhaps, with its Nazi backing and the flagrant disinclination of the rest of supposedly anti-fascist democratic Europe to support the Spanish Republic, it would have done so anyway. Ethel was witness to the subjugation of an ideal. What the Catalan people achieved in the mid 1930s is a potent reminder of the politically possible, more dreamed about than is readily admitted.

The position Ethel took, both during and after her journey to Spain, and the forces she sided with, are still matter for hot debate. Since the fall of the Soviet Union they are perhaps more relevant than ever. The Spanish war was pivotal in the ideological struggle that would decide the future – our present. It is often called the dress rehearsal for World War II, but it was even more than that. If the fascists had been defeated in 1939, and if the communists had not been the major force of Spanish resistance, our contemporary world might look very different.

Ethel lived on for another 23 years after her return. What she saw and reported on in Spain did not diminish either her resolve or her optimism for a better world. Far from seeing the betrayal of comrades and the triumph of the extreme right as a final defeat, she pointed to the profound changes that took place in Barcelona as proof of the need to fight on. In all her speeches, articles and tireless activities after the war, Ethel argued that what happened in Spain was a setback – a tragic and unnecessary one – but no more than that. Certainly not a final defeat.

# 1

## *La Dame aux Camélias*

*〜Despite all the forces that stand in our way, working people of true heart and real bravery will continue to fight for Justice and Equality . . . 〜*

Ethel opens a pack of ten Kensitas with one hand – a skill developed over years of dedicated smoking. She empties the entire packet onto the table, to save her the trouble of closing and re-opening the pack every ten minutes. With the other hand she keeps typing. One finger only, but fast. A cigarette card drops out of the pack, face down. She turns it, checks it, then skites it off her desk onto the pile of papers that surrounds a full wastepaper basket. It is a picture of the standard of HRH the Prince of Wales. Ethel has pinned a few others of the series on the notice-board behind her: the flag of the Irish Free State and the standard of Scotland. The Prince of Wales doesn't interest her. She lights a cigarette, keeps it in her mouth as she types.

August 1936. The small, dirty window looks directly across to another blackened Victorian building, just like the one Ethel is in. A shaft of sunlight falls between the two – compensation for the washout of summer so far. Wettest July on record. The noise from the street, two storeys below, seems to rise up that duct of light: tramcars, voices, the regular trains at the top of Queen Street, the low rumble of the subway deep below.

The Workers' Advice Centre consists of one cramped room with newspapers scattered everywhere and posters on the wall. One corner is stacked with reams of the latest edition of *Regeneración*. There is one scratched and bashed desk, clearly designed for a bigger and better space. Wedged amongst the clutter are three people: Ethel at the desk, concentrating on the case of a worker dismissed from Wills' cigarette factory; John, kneeling, ripping open the reams in the corner, the smell of crude new ink mingling with Ethel's smoke; Guy, as ever, on his feet, pacing, reading.

'They should have gone ahead.'

'Who should? With what?'

'The People's Olympiad.'

Ethel laughs. 'What? And bring more attention to Barcelona? Last thing they want.'

'I know we argued against the Olympics themselves,' says John from the corner, his accent an unblunted Ulster. 'But Jesse Owens!'

'And Cornelius Johnson!'

Guy turns the page of the *Glasgow Herald*. Ethel bows closer to the typewriter, trying to focus. Guy is incapable of reading any printed matter quietly.

'Miners in Jarrow are organising a march to Parliament. Much good it'll do them.'

'Can't not support it, Guy.' Ethel gives up typing. Guy puts the *Herald* down. 'Communist-backed.'

Guy Aldred has had a huge effect on Ethel's life: the latest influence in her development from an impassioned provincial girl to the dedicated activist she is now. Having worked closely – quite literally, given their lack of funds, in this tiny office – for several years, they behave like a married couple, except that Ethel is 27 years old, and Guy knocking on 50. He is wearing his trademark knickerbockers with gaudy socks and country-set tweed jacket. He is far from tall, but his energy and constant motion draw the eye. Even in bigger rooms, in halls, out in Glasgow Green, you couldn't ignore him. There is something of the evangelist about him – the gestures, the determined look in his eye, and when he speaks in public his voice dips and builds. The fact is, he once was a revivalist, 'The Holloway Boy Preacher'. His voice is deep brown, the Cockney accent not quite faded. He has lived an extraordinary life, first in the service of the Lord, then in the cause of the People.

Ethel is small too, and in contrast to Guy's constant motion, she sits still behind her desk, almost hidden by the massive, pre-war second-hand typewriter. But her stillness is intense. The smoke curls unflaggingly around her black hair, black suit, her dark, wide eyes. Her clothing is practical – a woollen two-piece for the Glasgow weather – but it fits well. The mix of forcefulness and patience about her give her grace, an allure.

The room seems as full as it can get, but the entire team isn't present yet. There is the sound of footsteps on the concrete stairs beyond the door, but none of the occupants looks round, well aware of who is about to enter. There is one other office on this landing, a property rental company. Most days there is a stream of people going in there, weeping, or swearing on their way back down. But these footsteps now belong to Jane Hamilton Patrick. John stands up and stretches his back. He is a little taller than his colleagues, his frame lean and solid from years of physical work. He's still not as tall as Jane, though, who comes in and sifts through the post she has picked up downstairs. All four exchange glances and quick smiles, the way people who have worked and socialised together constantly for a long time do. Ethel carries on typing; John organises his bundles; Guy reads.

Jenny, as Jane is known, coat still on, slim, her hair more up to date than Ethel's despite being older, methodically opens envelopes and discards them neatly into the bin by the desk. The scrawled handwritten letters are from clients, new or old, pleading for help. The smart typed ones are from employers, or the Corporation, or the police. Jenny puts them into separate bundles. There are also envelopes from political and social organisations – from people just like them across Britain. A third pile for those.

'The Jarrow petition.' Jenny's Irish accent is not as pronounced as John's.

'Leave it here, Jenny,' says Ethel. 'I'll get signatures when I'm out.'

Fifty years later, in his book *Come Dungeons Dark*, John Taylor Caldwell, out-surviving his three friends, wrote about what Guy really thought of the Hunger Marches of the 1930s: 'Stunts at the expense of the poor. Contrived by the leaders to advance their careers. They lead unemployed workers, ill shod, ill clothed, all the way to London, to stand cap in hand before the House of Commons.' Then again, Guy Aldred knew all about publicity, using the organs of the State to progress his cause. In years to come, he would present himself often for election to that House.

For the moment, he looks away from the petition and back at the typed document. 'Drawing-room prudes!'

He begins practising his defence for the woman at Wills' cigarette factory, laid off thanks to 'mechanisation'. Ethel knows from experience that Guy will address the case well, but will also use the opportunity to educate a roomful of confused managers on the bigger issues – which, to be fair, the case will marginally touch on. In particular, he will want to warn of the rise of fascism, and advocate free speech and sexual equality.

'You are in effect, gentlemen, managing a modern slave society!'

John unhooks his greatcoat from the back of the door. He first met Guy only a few weeks ago. He had given up seafaring and, in his own words a 'dreamy young man', he was looking for something more meaningful in his life. He immediately joined Guy's United Socialist Movement (USM). But he still looks for occasional work at the docks and shipyards to earn a few pounds for the communal coffers.

This quartet will work together for the next 25 years. John, 16 years younger than Guy but 3 years older than Ethel, will outlive them all and leave the best records we have of the USM's activities during an era of optimism and radicalism, of battles fought in the slums of Glasgow and the *barrios* of Barcelona.

Jenny has one last letter in her hand: from France, addressed to Guy. She leaves it on the corner of the desk. When he has stopped practising his argument for the Wills case, he will get round to reading it. It will change all of their lives – particularly Jenny's and Ethel's.

~

Freddie and May Turrell live in a pretty semi ten minutes' walk from number 309 Windmillhill Street. Their front room looks onto an autumn blaze of trees; four generations of family photographs hang on the walls. The history of Motherwell, of industrial Scotland, is there in the faces, suits and demeanour of grandparents, aunts and uncles, children and grandchildren.

'I was sitting watching telly,' May tells me, 'when this advert came on. I thought, "can't be", but I called in Freddie. "There's a programme starting on BBC about a Glasgow woman anarchist!"'

'We sat through it open-mouthed,' Freddie says. He is a tall man, fit and too young-looking to be several years retired. I search for an echo of Ethel in him, but can't see it. Ethel was small, dark, soft-featured. Freddie is chiselled, longer-faced. Perhaps he takes after the Turrell side. Later he shows me a photograph of his Macdonald granddad, and then I see the resemblance. If I had passed Freddie in the street, or on a train, I might have taken him for a Highlander. Not too far from the mark, as it turns out.

'We had no idea they were making a film about Auntie Ethel.' There is warmth and pride in his voice. 'We knew

6

most of the story, obviously, but that film had some details that were new to me.'

I already knew that Ethel had eight siblings: Freddie's aunts and uncles. He knew most of them personally, and was in regular touch with Carrie, the youngest of the family, until her death in America in June 2008.

'Of course, I only knew Auntie Ethel towards the end of her life. I wasn't even born when she was in Barcelona. My mother – Bessie, second youngest of the Macdonalds – used to take me to see her at her flat in Gibson Street. I was born in '44, and Ethel died in 1960. So I only knew her up to the age of 16.'

May, Freddie's wife, brings in coffee and cakes. *She* could sooner be Ethel's relative. Petite, welcoming and, like her husband, she smiles easily. 'She was always a presence in the family, Ethel. Even years later, when I came on the scene.'


For months I had been wondering about certain details on Ethel Macdonald's birth certificate, things that did not make sense to me. For instance, the fact, recorded in neat calligraphy, that her parents were married in Brentford. What were a Scottish working-class couple doing in London in 1901?

Ethel was born at home – 309 Windmillhill Street, Motherwell – at 3:30 a.m. on 24 February 1909. The tenement building no longer exists, but the street does, and is still the vital artery that links three old villages: Motherwell, Craigneuk and Wishaw, at the heart of Scotland's Steel Belt.

Her father was Andrew Macdonald. On Ethel's birth certificate he wrote – in his own hand – 'Coach Painter (Journeyman)'. That addition can only signal pride. He was fully apprenticed, in effect his own boss. Traditionally, tradesmen and guilds recognised three grades of worker – apprentices, journeymen and masters. In that middle category Andrew would have been independent. As we will see, he remained with the one employer for many years, but being a journeyman, he could, if he wished, up tools and find work elsewhere.

Ethel was the fifth child in a family of nine. First came Andrew junior, born just over six years before Ethel, who worked locally as a bus driver for most of his life. Next came Hugh, who emigrated to Canada early on and remained there. Next, Daisy, named after her mother, who worked for many years in Lewis's Department Store in Glasgow. The fourth child, Gordon, left home early, went to London where he eventually became a senior fireman, and met up from time to time with the next sibling down, Ethel.

The sixth was Ian, politically radical and, like Ethel, extremely well read. He served in the army, fought in Palestine, and ended his life carrying on a family tradition of working in transport – in his case an administrator for local buses. He was a neighbour of Freddie and May until his death two years ago. 'He was probably the brother closest to Ethel,' Freddie says. Fifty years after his birth he would sign his sister's death certificate.

Next came Elizabeth, or Bessie, Freddie's mum and Ethel's closest sister; then came Caroline. Better known as Carrie, she enacted the classic tale of meeting a GI during the war, marrying him, and going back to the States. Widowed, Carrie is now in South Carolina.

James, or Jimmy, was the youngest of the family – the

two children who followed him both died in infancy. Jimmy served with the police in East Kilbride. Freddie does not remember, or has never heard of, any bad feeling between Ethel and Jimmy despite his profession and the difficulties Ethel experienced with policemen in Spain. 'She was very fond of Charlie, too, Carrie's husband. Being an American soldier meant they sometimes had arguments, but it didn't stop Ethel from liking him.

'My memory of Ethel is of a quiet woman,' Freddie tells me. 'Warm. In a way she wasn't like the rest of the family who were . . .'

'Overpowering,' laughs May.

Freddie nods, but both agree that, as well as being talkative, the Macdonalds were a close family. 'Ethel went off and did her thing. Apart from the time she was in Barcelona, and before that in London and up north, she was just up the road in Glasgow. She wasn't around as much – at least not in my childhood – as the other family members who stayed here were. But there was never any falling-out. Auntie Ethel was just . . . wrapped up in her own world. Very busy.'

'Wasn't there a wee bit tension between Ethel and your grandmother?' May prompts him.

But Freddie changes the subject. 'You wanted to know why my grandfather got married in Brentford?'

The workforce 100 years ago was much more mobile than is generally thought. Journeymen got the name because they travelled from employer to employer and from place to place to earn their living. I had reckoned that the railway network, so important to both Motherwell and London, tied the two places together. Perhaps it was the rail companies that allowed Andrew to up sticks, work elsewhere for a period – and find himself a wife.

'So far as I know he never worked for a rail company,' Freddie says. 'I never knew my granddad. Died before I was born. We don't have documents to prove anything, but all the family grew up with granddad's story. He came down from Ballachulish on his own, at the age of 12. Not to Motherwell, but Paisley, to start his apprenticeship as a painter. When he completed it, he went to London looking for work.'

Rail-engine building employed a great number of men at that time. Not only for engines and carriages destined for the various British lines, but for everywhere in the Empire. 'Granddad stayed in digs in Brentford, and painted some of the first luxury railway coaches for India. He painted both the inside and the outside. Signage, varnishing, the lot.'

Yet all his children were born in Scotland. Andrew was not in Brentford for more than a couple of years. When he did return it wasn't to either Ballachulish or Paisley, but Motherwell. Presumably he heard of a job on offer there. Now a fully trained and experienced coach painter, he could find work easily in Scotland. John Taylor Caldwell, however, thought Ethel's dad had 'a peculiar job, which was becoming obsolete even then. He painted the gold and red lines around carriages, for the nobility. He'd paint monograms on the doors of the carriages. On horse-drawn carts, things like that.'

Eventually, Andrew found a position at Alexander's Buses that he stayed with for the rest of his life. Freddie tells me, 'I always remember my gran saying he used to paint the swallows that were the company's logo.'

No matter how short the stay in Brentford, it was of

crucial importance to Andrew's life – without it, Ethel and her brothers and sisters would never have been born. It was at the digs he lodged in that Andrew met his wife. 'They had to get married quickly,' according to May Turrell. When she sees my raised eyebrow, she adds, 'Not for that reason.'

'If you knew my grandmother, you'd understand,' said Freddie. 'The adjective everyone in the family uses to describe her is "Victorian". She was politically modern for the time, but certainly not morally. She would never have been so . . . *brazen*.'

Andrew married his landlady's daughter, Daisy Watts, on 26 August 1901. She was 16 years old. They were living in Motherwell for the arrival of their first-born, Andrew junior, in 1903.

'I remember Gran saying sadly that she never saw her mother again for 40 years.'

There was a detail on Ethel's birth certificate that had puzzled me. I pointed it out to Freddie. Andrew and Daisy Macdonald had not named their baby girl simply Ethel, but *Camelia* Ethel. Freddie had never noticed it, nor, he thought, was it general knowledge in the family. Other than Andrew and Daisy, only Ian, who signed her death certificate Camelia Ethel, had known her full name. Perhaps he may only have found out on that grim day.

Why Camelia? It is an unusual name. 'Ethel' at the time was popular enough: a sound, practical, no-nonsense name. Camelia, as it is spelled on the certificate, and the more common Camellia, are virtually unknown as Christian names, then as now. Camilla was just as rare. It must have had an odd resonance in industrial Lanarkshire in 1909 – perhaps why Ethel apparently dropped it as soon as she could.

Did Andrew and Daisy have a poetic streak to them? In Virgil's *Aeneid*, Camelia, or Camilla, is a fleet-footed warrior woman. The truth might be less exotic. Perhaps there were camellias in a nearby park, or in the gardens of rich folks' houses, and Ethel's parents liked them. Or Andrew painted a barge or trawler with the name – there are records of boats being named *Camelia*. Does it perhaps show an aspirational streak in the Macdonald family? Camelia sounds rather posh to us today and would have done so in 1909 too. But there was only one well-known Camelia around in those days: Camille, the protagonist of Alexandre Dumas's play *La Dame aux Camélias*.

If Andrew and Daisy had known the story would they have called their daughter after a high-class prostitute? The *dame* was a wilful, rambunctious, independent woman. In his 1853 opera, Verdi calls her La Traviata, or 'Fallen Woman'. It's a tempting – though no doubt idle – thought that in naming their daughter after a woman who refused to accept her fate, who challenged the norm and rejected dull bourgeois morality, Andrew and Daisy saw some glimmer of Camelia Ethel's future.

In any case, there must have been something about their latest arrival. When she was very little, Andrew nicknamed her 'Stormy Petrel'. The dizzying aerial displays of storm petrels and shearwaters can be seen off Scotland's west coast. They ascend and turn, hold the current, then break loose in a way that seems reckless to us but elementary to them.

~

Freddie changes from slippers into the sleekest and shiniest pair of black brogues, and the three of us set off in an equally sleek and shiny car. We head for Windmillhill Street.

There are remnants of the Steel Town, hiding between car showrooms, roundabouts, insurance offices, like shells on a pebble beach. Parts of the wall of the old Lanarkshire Steel Works still stand; in gaps between shops and offices you can glimpse the old Ravenscraig site – soon to become more shops and offices. The tower of the Dalzell plant sits glumly over the flat rooftops. We try and figure out where number 309 would have been. Nearly all the old tenements have been demolished, giving way to first 1920s then 1950s architecture, and later remodellings. A shame – they were lovely structures. Unlike Glasgow's, Motherwell's tenements, built of blond sandstone, rose only two, at most three, storeys high. One or two blocks remain, scrubbed up, with old-fashioned shops on the ground floor. I have a copy of Oliver van Helden's photograph book *Old Motherwell* on my lap, and I can recognise, through the window of Freddie's car, the type of house that Ethel would have lived in.

We find number 205, so hers must be a couple of blocks up. Finally, we decide that where the police station now stands could well have been number 309. We laugh at the irony.

Freddie points down a gap. 'Ravenscraig. Where I started my apprenticeship in 1960.' The same year his Auntie Ethel died. Freddie became a roll-turner, then he and May went off to South Africa for 11 years. 'Lovely place. Good job. But apartheid . . .'

There is a picture in the van Helden book of a street: a

line of low, two-storey tenements, not completely blackened yet by industrial smog. The text says the buildings were demolished by a tank during the Great War – an exhibition of Britain's military power. The event was part of a government fundraising campaign, selling war savings certificates. In the background there is a young girl – about the same age as Ethel would have been at the time. Maybe she witnessed the colonial show of strength.

Van Helden quotes a minister's account of the area 80 years previously in 1836: 'There are three villages in the parish, viz. Motherwell . . . Windmillhill, close to the church . . . and Craigneuk.' Ethel's older neighbours would have remembered the fruit-growing, weaving and handicrafts of a rural area. But there was coal too, and when the railway came in 1841, Motherwell's future was set in stone – or, rather, steel. In 1845 the West of Scotland Malleable Iron Company arrived in town. By 1896 – five years before Ethel's parents were married – 'the Malleable iron-works of the Glasgow Iron Company [were] the largest in Scotland', employing over 1,000 men. Motherwell was safely Scotland's steel capital. Skilled and unskilled workers were brought in from anywhere and everywhere. Andrew, Ethel's father, was one of them. This was his and Daisy's world. 'What was woods and fields has been covered with houses and works, which darken the air with smoke, and give the streets quite a Glaswegian aspect.'

There is another fascinating picture in *Old Motherwell*: two men on a Co-op steam-powered lorry. They are transporting what looks like beer or wine crates. The front of the iron-wheeled vehicle reads: 'Scottish Co-operative Wholesales.

95 Morrison Street, Glasgow.' Who knows, it could be in Andrew's hand.

A little nearer the centre, we come to the new premises – on the same site as the old building – of the *Motherwell Times*, an employer of Ethel's during the 1930s.

Next we head towards Bellshill. I had never understood why Ethel Macdonald was often called the Bellshill Anarchist in articles and headlines when she was clearly a Motherwell girl. To get there, we have to negotiate the one-way system and head a little back up Windmillhill Street towards Craigneuk. I tell Freddie and Ethel, in passing, that once, for a play I was writing, I wondered where the centre of Europe was. I got a map, decided where the continent's corners were. (Franz Josef Land, I think I went for, in the northwest; Istanbul, southwest, the Azores and somewhere in Iceland for the eastern frontiers. They're as good as any other four corners.) The epicentre of Europe, according to my rough Saltire cross, was Craigneuk. Audiences liked the joke. But actually, given the industry, the railways, aqueducts, the industrial history – Craigneuk's claim to the title isn't so ludicrous.

Freddie explains that the family moved, he isn't sure when, from 309 to 345. 'Maybe it was a bigger house. Or in better condition. But they didn't stay that long. They moved twice again.'

Motherwell was steel; Bellshill was coal. The homes on Milnewood Drive look to me like the 'homes fit for heroes' in the 1930s. Freddie stops the car and we sit outside the house Ethel returned to from her adventures in Barcelona. Pebbledash, modern-looking. We head off again for the last

Macdonald house, 133 Calder Road. In the distance stands a church, and I remember hearing a theory that a statue of an angel was built there in Ethel's honour. 'Seems unlikely,' says Freddie.

'Nobody in the family was religious?'

'Actually, yes. In fact, it runs through the family. But not your average Sunday-morning Kirk. My grandmother and some of her children were into Spiritualism.'

'Including your own mum, Fred,' says May. Ethel Macdonald, militant atheist and anarchist, with a Spiritualist younger sister.

In the early 1900s Spiritualism was already half a century old with roots going back another 150 years, but it was all the rage, particularly in London. Arthur Conan Doyle and Harry Houdini were famous believers. In Scotland, not so long before, Robert Owen, social reformer and founder of the Co-operative Movement, had been a firm Spiritualist and wrote extensively on the subject. Spiritualism had since its earliest days been closely associated with reform and radical thought. In part it was a reaction against the power of the established churches. Slavery abolitionists were often Spiritualists, and it appealed to women because it gave them a role – as mediums, and public speakers. A kind of new priesthood. Daisy was indeed very Victorian – but in some interesting ways. I also wonder if the name Camelia could have a Spiritualist, or Swedenborgian, association. Researching the idea later, I find no strong link.

What is becoming ever clearer is that Ethel came from a family of thinkers, socialists and strong women. Sitting in the car outside number 133 I could almost imagine her standing behind the net curtain. Freddie actually does remember her there. Andrew died while living in that house. Ian, the brother closest to Ethel, lived there till he died, too, only two years ago.

'We lived there, too' says May. 'When we got married, before we could afford a house of our own. With Daisy and Ian.'

'My aunt Ethel had passed away by then. Such a sad death. The irony of it. But I remember her being in there, visiting, with the rest of the family.'

The unguessable journeys of our lives: Freddie in South Africa; his uncle Jimmy in the police; Carrie still living in the States, an American soldier's widow. Driving back from Bellshill, May laughs and remembers a story. 'Freddie's mum always worried about her weight. She had no need to, but she did. She used to always tell the same story when the subject came up. Years ago – this would be in the forties? – she was here, at number 133. Ethel came in, and Bessie said she looked tremendous. "You've lost weight," Bessie said. "I went on a diet," Ethel replied. "That's it. I'm going on a diet too. First thing tomorrow." "No," said Ethel. "Start today."'

∽

The letter with a French postmark that arrived at the Workers' Advice Centre in Queen Street one October morning in 1936 was sent by André Prudhommeaux.

Prudhommeaux was a French anarchist who had just returned to Paris after some months in Barcelona. He had witnessed two historic processes – the developing revolution in Barcelona and the early days of the Spanish Civil War.

Monarchist and right-wing generals had rebelled against

17

the democratically elected Republic two months before he wrote to Guy Aldred. Guy had already made the generals' rebellion and the defence of the Republic the centre of all his speeches, at political meetings, in the streets, and on Glasgow Green. The revolution taking place in Barcelona, Madrid and Aragon was, he wrote in August 1936 'the mighty proletarian movement that Europe needed'. John Taylor Caldwell later remembered that those speeches 'drew bigger crowds than at any time since the general strike'. A fortnight after the outbreak of war, Ethel and Guy had produced the first copy of their United Socialist Movement's newssheet, *Regeneración*.

Ethel immediately set to work on writing up Prudhomm-eaux's appeal for arms and money and soldiers to support the Barcelona anarchists, and for their activities and ideals to be publicised in Britain. Guy Aldred began planning a USM/Anti-Parliamentary expedition of volunteers. In his letter, Prudhommeaux suggested that a writer and activist be sent from Britain to report back on the extraordinary events unfolding in Spain.

Everyone knew of the political situation in Spain, of the right wing's advances from the south of the country. Few, though, realised what was happening in the streets of Barcelona and in the villages and fields of Catalonia and Andalusia, that there might be much bigger implications for Europe than merely a war between left and right. Anti-authoritarians and revolutionaries were creating the first shoots of an entirely new society, never experienced anywhere in the world before. To go to Barcelona in 1936 was to see the formation of an entirely new world.

Guy was needed here in Glasgow; John was too new to the Movement and had no experience in writing. Prudhommeaux had no money to offer and the USM would find it difficult enough to raise the funds to send one of their number to Spain – let alone a unit of fighting men. Although Ethel was showing promise as a political writer and her dedication was beyond question, Jenny Patrick must have been the leading candidate: she was a central figure in the Glasgow Anarchist Group, closely attached to Aldred both personally and politically – she and Guy were often described as 'partners' – and, in 1936, had a much higher profile than the relative newcomer Macdonald. Guy, however, for various reasons felt that Ethel might be the better choice.

# 2

# *Revolution in the Air*

∾ *It may take a decade or less – it may take a century
– or more – but come it will. The human spirit will not
allow itself to be squashed and imprisoned forever.* ∾

Ethel stood outside Glasgow City Chambers, selling copies
of *Regeneración*; this edition contained a plea for funds for
the planned USM/A-PCF expedition to Spain: 'Many
readers could help us. Some could advance all the money
needed. The delegation must leave within one week. Will
comrades make a special effort, by loans and donations? If
this delegation and expedition is delayed unduly, the Anti-
Parliamentarians will prove themselves to be as contemptible
as Parliamentarians.'

Ethel didn't need to go all the way to Barcelona for
everyday drama. Standing in the centre of George Square,
she saw office workers rushing to tea-rooms and pubs for
lunch that had to be ordered, consumed and paid for within
half an hour. Ethel knew all about tea-rooms – her meteoric
career in Lyons' Corner Houses in London only a few years

ago had resulted in her first bitter clash with management. She knew the conditions, the pay, and the powerlessness of the women and girls who served tables.

Looking east towards Duke Street, she saw workers changing shifts at the cigarette factory and the tram and train works. The dirty, wearied ones still with a spring in their step because their day's work was done. The sprucer ones quiet, just about to start. Along Queen Street men from another shift were crossing paths, on their way back to or from the Clyde. Riveters, boilermakers, platers, unskilled labour. She knew the geography of the city like her own reflection in a mirror. Dixon's Blazes and the inferno of their forges southwest; northeast, Cowlairs and the railway works; around the city, farms where families desperately eked a living out of a dying culture.

Glasgow had all the drama a city could ever offer: work, drink, laughter, sex, anger. And gang warfare. Only last year an innocent passerby was stabbed to death when rival gangs clashed in the Gorbals. The Derry Boys, the Norman Conks, the – poetically named – Savoy Arcadians. Billy Boys attacked Catholic schools; Celtic fans fought with Rangers fans. The Orange Walk. Hibernian marches. The divisions among the working class pained her deeply, although she understood the causes. Years of unions and progress ruined by starving people seeking work from another part of Great Britain. Ethel could never see what was so great about it.

Nearly a quarter of this city's population were in receipt of public assistance relief; over 100,000 were long-term unemployed. The City Fathers, housed in the sumptuous Victorian chambers behind her, were reducing dole payments at a time when Glaswegians had never been so poor – the majority of them anyway. The big houses peered down from Park, or hid between lines of trees south and west of the river. Ethel not only knew about the battles that sent fault lines all through her adopted city, she was on the frontline of many of them.

Just recently, 1,000 people reacted as one, attempting to rescue a man who had been arrested by the police. She knew more than most people did about the mystery bomb that damaged the army recruiting office in Bath Lane last year – and she didn't approve. Not even a fully paid-up member of the Glasgow Anarchist Group would endorse bombings like that – despite how the popular press liked to portray anarchists. No one had been hurt, but such acts were random, pointless. Peace and a peaceful route to it were the ideal, though if the enemies of working people gave them no other option, Ethel had no qualms about fighting.

She had visited the 'Nomads' – young men and women denied benefits thanks to the hated Means Test – a cause taken up by Jimmy Maxton, who Ethel would later meet, far from home. These dispossessed lived in woods and hills around the city, unwittingly, for the most part, experimenting with a new way of living, another kind of society. Right now there were plans afoot to organise training camps for anyone thinking of going to Spain to fight. But therein lay another division – between the communists and people like Ethel, revolutionaries suspicious of parliaments, fighting over who should run the camps.

The world was in flux. Mussolini, Hitler, now the Spanish generals. In this country, Mosley's blackshirts were gaining strength. It astounded some, but was obvious to Ethel, that a supposedly respectable daily newspaper like the *Mail* could be openly supportive of fascism and all that it entailed: anti-semitism, racism, tyranny, hatred of the common man disguised as adoration. The dictators' misuse of the word 'socialism' infuriated her, as it did every humane and thinking person. The British government's appeasement of such men surprised her not in the least. In public it denounced the German and Italian regimes, and now spoke out against the Spanish Falangists, but it offered no support to the Republic. Forced to choose between fascists for neighbours, or communists, or worse still, revolutionaries seeking a genuinely democratic state, of course the government would rather the dictators. In her youth an ardent Labour supporter, it had cost Ethel to realise that no party in Parliament would ever push for radical reform.

Communism was, to Ethel's mind, showing its true colours. Stalin was at this moment 'trying' Zinoviev and Kamenev, claiming that, conspiring to restore capitalism, they had plotted to assassinate him. To Ethel this was merely Stalin consolidating personal power, betraying everything the Russian Revolution had stood for. It saddened her to see Harry Pollitt, a man she once admired, write in the *Daily Worker*: 'the trials in Moscow represent a new triumph in the history of progress'.

In Ethel's mind it was clear: there were not *two* battles – one against the vile spectre of the extreme right and another within the left. There was one: against totalitarianism, however it dressed itself up, a struggle for progress and justice. That did not mean lumping all those forces together – the Nazis and the right were the clear enemy. Parliamentary socialists, communists and left-leaning liberals meant well. But everything she had experienced, all the thought and discussion she had put into politics, told her they were wrong, and that their ideals could be so easily corrupted.

How could a woman like Ethel Macdonald end up fearing socialists and communists? They were her brothers, sisters, parents, all the people she had grown up with and loved, who had helped form her, brought her to the place she now was.

A man, dressed in a suit, bought one of her papers. She would never be able to compete with the Communist *Daily Worker*, which had sold 2,000 copies of its Spain Special in a single night. The United Socialist Movement had nothing like the CPGB's money and infrastructure. Still, one copy was enough to raise spirits.

And now it looked like she herself might be going to Spain. To a city she had been reading about for over a year, where a genuine revolution was in full flight.

Jenny Patrick was at this very moment talking to her anarchist comrades. Ethel would have to wait and see what happened there. What an education it would be to see what was happening in Catalonia; what a privilege to play a small part in the construction of a new world – and just as the fascists were attacking. But if they decided that Jenny was the best person to go, Ethel would accept it; the main thing was the revolution's success. Whether she or Jenny Patrick witnessed what was going to happen was of no importance whatsoever. She held *Regeneración* up higher and called louder. She was doing swift business today.

～

Ethel Macdonald's homeland, Lanarkshire, was the cauldron of industrial Scotland. It was in New Lanark that David Dale teamed up with Richard Arkwright, inventor of the water frame for cotton spinning. Tunnels and canals were built to drive the water to their machines – some important first steps towards a factory society.

James Watt graduated from Glasgow University. He modified the steam engine, increasing its industrial potential. Coal, essential to Central Scotland's development, could now be mined faster, deeper and more efficiently in Lanarkshire and beyond. The introduction of the Monklands – and later, the Forth and Clyde – canals increased production exponentially. Henry Bell in 1812 built the world's first commercially viable steamship, the *Comet*. Carron Ironworks was Scotland's first large coke-smelting plant. In Motherwell itself, the first ironworks opened in 1871 and became the country's largest steel producers.

All this was caused by, and in turn created, massive social upheaval, with overcrowding, unemployment, bad housing and poverty. The world of Andrew and Daisy Macdonald, and of Ethel as a child, was one of endless moral panics over workers' drinking and lack of religion. Employers and unions battled it out, pitching profit against living wages and reasonable working conditions. Irish immigration caused dissent amongst the lower orders. Motherwell, like all the growing towns and cities forged in the industrial revolution, threw out a scalding political heat.

But Lanarkshire had also long been a progressive centre for political and social experiment. When Robert Owen fell in love with David Dale's daughter and settled in New Lanark, he bought four textile factories there and experimented with early liberal-minded ideas. Convinced that the environment in which people live impacts fundamentally on their nature and wellbeing, he built better housing for his employees, constructed schools and raised the employment age from six to ten. He reduced the length of the working day, prohibited physical punishment which was common in factories, and wrote several books on his theories, hoping to influence other industrialists and employers. He was an atheist who believed in the possibility of a 'new moral world, a world from which the bitterness of divisive sectarian religion would be banished'. He would have been well discussed in the Macdonald household, not only for his political progressiveness, but for his allegiance to Spiritualism.

During the course of Ethel's parents' lives, a political theory and practice was taking shape that went far beyond the patrician charitableness of Owen and Dale. Andrew Macdonald's birth date is unknown, but it cannot have been much earlier or later than 1883, the year Karl Marx died. In 1895, when Andrew would have been beginning his apprenticeship, Friedrich Engels, having long before witnessed first-hand in his father's Manchester factory the deplorable conditions of the British working class, died whilst still translating Marx's writings.

The ideas these two men explored and sought to make reality – ideas which long pre-existed them, but which they brought together in a powerful form – would shape the future of the world, and have a massive impact on Ethel's life. From Engels in particular, Ethel's ideas of the role of women in society were formed. Engels proposed that in the same way as the bosses and the State controlled workers' lives, male and religious institutions – including marriage – oppressed women.

Ethel was a voracious reader and undoubtedly read everything Marx wrote. She called herself a Marxist throughout her life and acted in accordance with his socialist theories. However, the sheer depth and expanse of Marx's theories inevitably leave them open to interpretation, particularly with the passing of time. A central, contentious issue within Marxism was already being debated as far back as the 1860s. At the First International, the earliest major meeting and organisation Marx presided over, there was a furious debate between his own supporters and those behind Mikhail Bakunin, who represented the anarchist wing.

'According to the theory of Mr Marx,' Bakunin wrote, 'the people not only must not destroy [the State] but must strengthen it and place it at the complete disposal of their benefactors, guardians, and teachers – the leaders of the Communist Party . . . who will proceed to liberate [mankind] in their own way. They will concentrate the reins of government in a strong hand, because the ignorant people require exceedingly firm guardianship.'

The argument – then, as now, and in Spain in 1936 – was over the transition from capitalism to communism proper. Marx and Engels argued that a temporary stage, the dictatorship of the proletariat, was necessary, elevating the working class into the ruling class; only after that would the State wither away. Bakunin's disagreement with that – 'freedom can be created only by freedom' – earned Marx's scorn.

27

He claimed that the anarchist wing's programme was 'a superficially scraped-together hash of Right and Left'. Bakunin's writings, he noted, 'found favour in Italy and Spain, where the real conditions of the workers' movement are as yet little developed, and among a few vain, ambitious and empty doctrinaires.'

Marx won out, and Bakunin was expelled from the First International at the Hague Congress in 1872. But Bakunin's ideas lived on, both within and outwith the Second International, and in the division in the twentieth century between Lenin and Trotsky.

Ethel, from the beginning of her writing, was very much on the revolutionary, anarchist-tinged side of that debate. Guy Aldred later wrote of two communisms: 'an authoritarian communism that would persecute like an autocratic State' and 'a free communism'.

Industrial Central Scotland was a key centre for the creation of the British Labour Party. Many of its protagonists were Scots: Kier Hardie, Maxton, Maclean, Cunninghame Graham. This last had been a Liberal MP for Northwest Lanarkshire, and the first to call himself a socialist in the House of Commons. He had been arrested in 1887's 'Bloody Sunday', when police brutally intervened in a free-speech demonstration. The aristocrat's subsequent imprisonment and outspokenness had made him a fok hero in Scotland.

The grudgingly conceded Representation of the People Act in 1884 gave more working people the opportunity to use democratic political action to further their interests. Kier Hardie's Mid-Lanark Alliance was the springboard, in 1888, well within Andrew's lifetime, for the Scottish Labour

Party. Lanarkshire was once again at the centre of a new political world. In 1893 Scottish Labour merged with the Independent Labour Party, and the unions joined them in 1899. In 1909 – the year Camelia Ethel was born – the Labour Party as we know it was formed.

Ethel Macdonald grew up with discussions, arguments, plans and disagreements. A plethora of working men's organisations operated in the industrial centres: communists, socialists, social democrats. Andrew, Daisy and the entire family could hardly have helped being immersed in the debates and activities that raged around them. As a child, Ethel saw banners and posters, heard of neighbours and family being laid off, listened to the debates on street corners.

Anarchism in Scotland was stronger than is now generally realised. There were groups in Paisley, Dundee and Glasgow. Alongside, and emanating from, the wider Marxist and socialist debate, were radical thinkers of a different ilk. Take, for instance, the two Tom Bells. The more famous of the two now is the Tom Bell who was one of the founders of the Communist Party in Scotland. The other was Thomas Hastie Bell, friend of the extraordinary Scots thinker, Patrick Geddes. Hastie Bell disagreed with the notion of using parliament as a tool towards socialism – another dividing line between communists and anarchists. Bell was a member of the Socialist League, first formed in London in 1884, whose members included William Morris and, initially, though she was opposed to the anarchists, Marx's daughter, Eleanor. The League was committed to the ideal of revolutionary internationalism, a cause Ethel Macdonald would later take up. They ran a successful branch in Glasgow, and became a springboard for Scottish anarchists.

The term 'anarchism' was associated with as much controversy and fear in the nineteenth and twentieth centuries as Islamicism is now. The word itself derives from the Greek *arkhos,* ruler, and the prefix *an-,* without: a social theory that aims for the dismantling of political domination. Since 1894, 'anarchists' had assassinated four European leaders – the president of France, the empress of Austria, the king of Italy, and the prime minister of a country that was going to play a central role in Ethel's life – Spain. The royal family of that same country were attacked by a bomb hidden under their royal carriage. Nearer home, two years after her birth, the Prince of Wales sustained two gunshot wounds from a 16-year-old calling himself an anarchist. In 1911 in London, much hyped in the press, was the siege of Sydney Street. A decade before Ethel was born – but surely still a talking point during her childhood – a bomb exploded in a bank in Motherwell. A theory went round that the money was used to fund the assassination of President McKinley in 1901.

These events were all very different, but they were conveniently lumped together by the popular press and tagged under the heading 'anarchism', creating the absurd villainous stereotype that remains with us even now. Like Islamicism today, anarchism was a tag that disenfranchised and disorganised groups – and dysfunctional individuals – found convenient. This, however, was not Ethel's anarchism, or Bakunin's.

~

Freddie Turrell, the day he took me through Motherwell and his aunt's past, stopped at Knowetop Primary School, just a few streets from where he now lives.

'I imagine she must have gone to school here. My mother, who was only a few years younger, did. So did Aunt Carrie.'

It's a Victorian building, standing next to the Davie Cooper Stand of Motherwell FC's Firpark ground. Although we're not far from Windmillhill Street, where remnants of the past are left only in forgotten corners, outside Knowetop Motherwell's history is palpable. The stand is actually a 1990s construction, but there's something timeless about football stadia. Cooper himself was a Lanarkshire boy, from just up the road in Hamilton. He was a Rangers legend as well as a Motherwell one: one of those players who sum up not only the decades in which they achieved success, but also the 100 years of working-class history preceding them. Freddie is a Motherwell fan. We don't know if Andrew was, though the club was formed just before he settled in the area.

'My grandson, Calum, goes to this school now. Seems it's a family tradition.'

May has tracked down a reference to Ethel in Knowetop Primary's records. It's interesting. On 1 September 1919 there is an entry showing that Ethel Macdonald, daughter of Andrew Macdonald, left the school. This would have been just before her tenth birthday. It gives the domicile as 307 Cadzow – an address not mentioned anywhere else in Ethel's story. Under 'Reason for Leaving' is written the word 'England'. We can only assume that, for some reason, Ethel, perhaps with her father or with one or more of her older siblings, went to stay with Daisy's family in London. A second record shows that she returned to school at the start of the winter term on 12 January 1920. She had been away from Glasgow for four months. The address she returned to is 307 Windmillhill Street. Both addresses can only be inaccurate – Andrew and Daisy were almost certainly at 309 Windmillhill Street during this period.

We head now to Dalzell Secondary, the school Freddie reckons Ethel most likely attended after Knowetop. He knows for certain that several of her brothers and sisters went there. It's a rather grand building. Get the camera angle right and you could set an Edwardian Charterhouse School drama in it. Long, low, castellated, it was opened in 1898, so must have had a new, modern feel to it when Ethel attended. Others in the family, however, went to Brandon High School, or Bellshill Academy. None of the three has any record of either an Ethel Macdonald or a Camelia Ethel on their books. She seems to have disappeared from educational history. Perhaps she left as soon as she could, sensing how unimportant girls' education was considered to be.

Everyone says Ethel did well at school. John Taylor Caldwell mentions the fact several times; it crops up in articles and obituaries. It's lore amongst the Macdonald family: Ethel was bright – academically as well as politically. Of course, there's a tendency to make such claims when there's lack of evidence. We imagine that someone who does well later in life must have been a good scholar as well.

If one family story indicates Ethel's promise it was the lifelong tension between herself and her mother. Daisy had big plans for Ethel and, although they never came to falling out over it, she had hoped her daughter would 'do well' in the conventional sense. During high school Ethel was sent for elocution lessons. The already politicised young Ethel might well have resisted such an aspirational move – though it would pay off wonderfully in ten years' time in Barcelona. Daisy seems to have made a special case of her fifth child, in educational terms at least, and she must have based that on some proven ability.

'I think my grandmother dreamt of a parliamentary career for Ethel. Not just for her own good, but for what she could achieve for families like theirs.'

Ironic, then, that Ethel had little faith in the parliamentary system. At 16 she joined the Youth Movement of the Independent Labour Party, positioned on the revolutionary left, and soon after became branch secretary.

The women in Ethel's early life would have cooked and cleaned all day long, for families of up to ten children. Many took part-time work to supplement their husbands' paltry wages – cooking and cleaning again for the families of the rich. Domestic treatment of women was not much better than that of the State's for its workers. While Ethel was still growing up, her future colleague Guy Aldred was speaking out against society's treatment of women. 'For a thousand years the insane and inane denunciation of women has been the teaching of Christendom . . . The function of women is not to share barracks with man and bear his children!'

The deplorable conditions and lack of housing in particular mobilised Scottish women. Before and after the Great War many became active in local tenants' associations, which led them to contribute to the wider political debate. The Glasgow Women's Housing Association, Women's Labour

League, Women's Freedom League and the Women's Social and Political Union all became important political groups. Ethel must have heard these voices and realised early in life that a radical change had to come in women's lives.

She had heroines to learn from at the time. Twenty years before her birth, Emmeline Pankhurst had formed the Women's Franchise League. By the time Ethel was born, its successor, the Women's Social and Political Union, was highly active and creating headlines. Ethel was only five when Emily Davidson threw herself in front of King George's horse, but the continuing passion and determination of the suffragettes must have been hugely impressive to Ethel's young, political mind. When war broke out, female family and friends in Motherwell would have taken over men's jobs in the factories, and been promptly thrown back out again when peace was declared. Perhaps Ethel was less taken by Christabel Pankhurst's distribution of white feathers to civilian men. When the Representation of the People Act gave the vote only to women over 30, Ethel would have felt the disappointment and anger around her.

Ethel Macdonald would be the first to remind us that she was a product of her time. Hers were not the politics of the individual, the exception: any young, thinking person, living in the world she lived in would be aware of and interested in that world, and feel a desire to affect it. In the years immediately before the Great Depression when unemployment levels were rising steeply, Ethel, like most of her friends and family, would have been involved at a local level.

Regardless of how well she might have done at school, there was precious little opportunity for women to continue into higher education in the early 1920s, even less for working-class women from Scotland's industrial belt. According to John Taylor Caldwell, she 'worked in a wee newsagent's shop when she left school. She was an assistant there when she was 14.'

That same story is mentioned by others and crops up several times in interviews and in writing by Caldwell. But Freddie Turrell has a lot more light to shine on his aunt's history.

Between school and leaving for London around 1927 had been the 'mysterious years' in Ethel's life. After our first meeting, Freddie asks around members of the family in various parts of Scotland and further afield. Slowly, a whole new story begins to emerge. What he finds out is dramatic, and changes our understanding of Ethel and the woman she became.

She did work in a newsagent's – but not until after she had gone 'north' – variously described by family members as 'the Highlands' and 'the northwest' – to work in a hotel. Perhaps she returned to her ancestral Ballachulish. She was away for, at the very least, a year. She waitressed and then tended bar – a profession that did not go down well with her 'Victorian' mother.

Not only that, but she met the love of her life.

'We don't know his name, nor how exactly they met,' Freddie says. But all the family knew of very real letters which went between the two when Ethel later returned home. 'When she did come back, she was distressed. And pregnant.' It's believed the man was an American merchant seaman – though what he'd be doing in the West Highlands, we don't know. 'But he was married. Ethel said so.'

The couple had declared their love. He went back to the States, but then – an old story – finally wrote to say he couldn't bring himself to leave his wife. It is pretty certain that he knew about Ethel's pregnancy, but it was not enough to persuade him.

It was always felt that Ethel had been deeply in love with her American sailor. She didn't seem bitter about his final decision; saddened rather, and no doubt rejected. As we'll see in later chapters, Ethel never became antagonistic to men in general – on the contrary, she enjoyed male company, and in every sense. But she never again trusted a relationship and avoided putting herself in the position of being let down and betrayed again.

On Ethel's return to the family home, from what we know of Daisy it is unlikely that the news of her daughter's condition went down lightly. But the Macdonalds were a close and supportive family. Ethel moved back in, and her parents, brothers and sisters looked after her during her pregnancy. When her time came, she was taken to Bellshill Maternity Hospital. Sadly, she miscarried. Daisy took her home from hospital, and she stayed with the family in Milnewood Drive. However, whereas when Ethel was pregnant, her mother had been caring and forgiving, she began now to be more oppressive of her wayward daughter.

'She kept her on a tight rein,' says Freddie. 'Reins and Auntie Ethel don't go well together.'

It was now that Ethel found the job at the newsagent's, not, as Caldwell thought, straight after school. Knowing how determined and independent Ethel was, how big her political vision would soon become, working in a shop and going home to her mother's suspicious gaze must have been soul-destroying. Her meetings at the ILP would have sated part of her desire for a bigger world and a broader view of life, but not enough to make her domestic situation tolerable.

Her sister Carrie remembers that one day, instead of going to work, Ethel, now in her very late teens, simply packed a bag and, with barely a word to anyone, left.

Where she went at first is uncertain – perhaps to see the cousins in London she had visited as a ten-year-old. Freddie believes she was in Glasgow first for a while and, in fact, met Guy Aldred there for the first time, around 1927 or '28. She might even have told him of her plan to go to London, and Aldred might have promised to get friends to help her if she did. Other reports, however, claim that Ethel and Guy did not know one another until her return from the capital.

From here, John Taylor Caldwell picks up the story. He gets the dates wrong, thinking Ethel got the job at the shop immediately after school, but his account of her arrival and experiences in London is the only one we have, and, dates aside, fits with family memories and friends' accounts. Still, it's interesting that Caldy – as he was universally known – made that mistake. Generally, when he spoke about Ethel he relayed what she told him. So either Ethel never mentioned the love affair, the pregnancy and the miscarriage, or Caldy himself decided to gloss over the story. The first seems the most likely as Caldwell was a progressive man of the left, and would have seen no shame in any part of her story. But Ethel kept her private life to herself and, as we'll see, her relationship with Caldy was complex. If she did fail to tell him the whole story, it was either out of hurt or a determination to control her own life, not out of shame.

'She was working in the newsagent's and she thought – I'm worth something better than this,' Caldwell said. 'She and a pal went down to London.'

There is no other mention anywhere of this friend. The family had never heard anything about her going to London with someone else. But we can only stick to Caldy's story as he told it.

'The impression I got from her was that it was just a 16-year-old tiff, a huff.' We know now, of course, that she was 18 at the very least. '"Well," she said, "I'm just going away." So she and this other girl about her own age, they must have hitchhiked to London. And they got there at 12 o'clock at night, wandering round the streets. They didn't know where to go or what to do, until a big policeman, a sergeant, came across and asked them what they were doing. They said they had come to London to look for work. And he said, "Silly girls, you silly girls." But he took them into a residential square with fancy motor cars and opened one of the big car doors and put them both in. And he gave them his piece – there were no canteens in those days, policemen carried their pieces with them. "Now you stay there until the morning and you'll be safe enough," and he shut them in. So they slept there for the night.'

But where did they sleep the next night? There's the possibility that she had already met Guy Aldred and had contacts from him. Caldwell did not know where Ethel stayed during all her time in London. She would have eventually found digs. No one can put precise dates on her arriving and leaving London, but she must have stayed for a year at the very least, perhaps as many as four. According to John Caldwell, she found a job as a waitress in a Lyons' Corner House teashop. 'She must have separated from her friend as she never spoke of her to me again. She talked about getting a succession of jobs as a waitress and she worked her way to a kind of head waitress situation.'

Lyons' chain of teashops – one of the founders of which was Nigella Lawson's grandfather – were opening up venues all over the capital. As well as tea and scones, they often organised tea dances, live music and theatrical events. Caldwell remembers Ethel telling him that her first romantic encounter (the first as far as he knew, or was prepared to say) was with a fellow worker. 'A young man in the vegetable room. He had a liking for classical music which he introduced her to. Was very fond of passing records on to her. But she seemed then to have a quarrel with him.'

Caldwell was very elderly when he recounted what had been told to him so long before, and it's possible he got two stories mixed up. The man in question may have been Ethel's boss, and she was soon more than quarrelling with him. Ethel was given a promotion at Lyons; according to Caldwell, she 'was the boss girl' and went 'round the hotels with holiday makers', presumably as a kind of tour guide for Lyons guests. But then the manager – whom Caldwell suggests was the same man she had been friendly with – told her she would only be paid 16 shillings, more or less what she had been earning before. Men in the same post got 18 shillings; she was outraged and had a terrible row with him.

Another betrayal; but Ethel was never one to be injured and defeated. She learned. This was a lesson in power in all its various forms, in the personal sphere, more often than not male controlling female, and in the workplace. Her experiences at Lyons, both personal and professional, wove their way into her political thought. As another character in her story, one whom we will meet later, said, 'Loyalty, honesty, those are the basic values of anarchism . . . Not to be subservient but to fight to become decent people.'

Either Lyons dismissed Ethel or she left. The date of her departure from London is uncertain, but we know she returned to Glasgow.

'She came back,' Caldwell says, 'because she had no money.' She never would have money, and she would find herself penniless in far more dangerous surroundings in the future.

~

'*Regeneración*! New edition!'

Ethel pronounced it 'regeneration'. She knew a few Spanish slogans. *'No Pasarán!' 'Ayuda España!' 'Victoria – hoy más que nunca!'* She printed Republican posters in her magazine, and learned the phrases from there. It is a language she was always going to find difficult. But she knew just enough to give her magazine a Spanish name. *Regeneración* – rebirth, renewal.

'Find out about the Spanish workers' revolt!'

She sold enough copies to know that there was interest and a thirst for new possibilities and a better society, though not enough to pay for the paper and printing – or wages, but that was not the point. Personal wealth had never been an option in Ethel's life, or an aspiration. The only thing on her mind now, apart from selling her paper – trying as ever to get the people around her to see that they *could* have strength and power – is what would happen over Prudhommeaux's invitation to Spain.

Guy seemed convinced that Ethel herself would be the ideal emissary from the Scottish left to go and report from Barcelona. Ethel wrote well, campaigned assiduously and was thoughtful and dedicated. She had a way with people, including those outside the radical left. She too had to admit that her experience of life to date had prepared her well for this mission. Perhaps it had all led up to this one, crucial challenge.

# 3

# *The Guy They All Dread*

*∽ English-speaking workers! Why are you sleeping while your Spanish brothers and sisters are being murdered? Where are your traditions? Speak! Act! ∽*

Guy Aldred had lived through, and taken vocal part in, almost every political debate since the dawn of the century. By the time Ethel met him he was a legendary figure in Glasgow, making impassioned speeches on street corners and on Glasgow Green and known as 'the Knickerbocker Rebel'.

Guy Aldred was born in London in 1883. It was religion, not politics, that first inspired him. By the age of 15 he had gained a reputation as a boy preacher, handing out his own Christian leaflets which were often received with ridicule. He preached in London's worst slums, and it was there, among the capital's poorest, that he first became interested in 'freethinking'. That led, in time, to his conversion to agnosticism. His work in the poorest parts of London brought him into contact with the ideas of socialists and revolutionists, particularly that of the artist, architect, writer and translator

William Morris. Morris had been a Liberal but his socialist thinking stemmed from his direct connection with Marx and Engels. He disagreed with them, however, over the principle of democratic centralism. 'State socialism?' he wrote in 1890, 'the two words contradict one another.'

Aldred became friendly with William Stewart Ross – a curious Scotsman who, decades earlier, had travelled a similar intellectual road to Aldred. Ross had been studying for the ministry at Glasgow University when he decided that he was more of a rationalist than a theist. In the 1880s he set up and edited *The Secular Review,* often writing under the name of 'Saladin' – quite an aggressive anti-Christian nom de plume, invoking the scourge of the Crusaders. Ross, amongst other political and social interests, wrote extensively, if rather romantically, about the power of women, and through him Aldred became involved in rationalist debates, feminism and politics – Scottish politics in particular.

A poem, 'Meditation', written by Aldred, quoted by Caldwell, shows how he used some of the language of faith in his politics, perhaps retaining some seeds of his youthful devotion:

> *To the destiny of man,*
> *To the instinct of my own nature,*
> *To the martyred spirit of all dead pioneers,*
> *Let me pray.*

Buddhism also interested him. For years, Edwin Arnold's poem, 'The Light of Asia', the story of the Buddha, lay on his desk. One verse is underlined:

*We are the voices of the wandering wind,*
*Which moan for rest and rest can never find;*
*Lo! As the wind is, so is mortal life,*
*A moan, a sigh, a sob, a storm, a strife.*

Guy considered many kinds of responses to oppression and poverty, from social democracy to communism, but finally settled on the revolutionary left. He read Bakunin and agreed that authority itself must be challenged. In the first decade of the twentieth century, he published a series of *Pamphlets for the Proletarians*, in one of which he asked 'Was Marx an anarchist?'

Aldred's thinking on feminism and male power brought him to believe that marriage was a male form of institutional oppression, and it was as an advocate of 'free love' that Guy Aldred first hit the headlines. We should remember that that term had different connotations at the turn of the twentieth century than it does today. Aldred's thinking on the matter would be nearer to William Stewart Ross's and Robert Owen's than to, say, Allen Ginsberg's and the counter-culturalists of the 1950s and 1960s, the focus more on eliminating the State's and the Church's involvement in any personal contract between a man and woman, than on the right to multiple partners or promiscuity. Aldred, however, would have defended any person's right to love whomsoever they wished.

His partner from 1907 was Rose Witcop. They were not married, and had a son, Annesley. Unlike Emmeline Pankhurst, Aldred was a conscientious objector during World War I – serving a prison sentence as a result. Rose's cause célèbre was family planning and birth control, and for their speeches and writings on these subjects they were both arrested. The government tried to silence Rose by threatening to deport her – Rose, née Rachel Vitkopski, was Jewish and born in the Ukraine. Deportation was avoided by her marriage – after, in fact, they were estranged – to Guy.

Aldred was next in trouble over a different matter. Naturally an exponent of Home Rule and dismantling of the colonial system, he was arrested for publishing an article by Shyamji Krishnavarma. The Indian nationalist's writings had already been legally declared seditious and were banned; Aldred published the article under his own name, which earned him twelve months' hard labour.

His connections with Scotland were cemented when the Clarion Scouts invited him to speak in Glasgow. The Scouts were a youth socialist pioneer group, a progressive take on Christian Fellowships. Launched in the last decade of the nineteenth century, they organised bike rides in the country, camping trips, weekend activities, all of which ultimately led to the formation of Socialist Sunday Schools. At the time they were not allied to any particular party, but worked with the ILP and anarchists alike. The Scouts invited Guy to speak in 1912, and he attracted such a crowd and enthusiastic responses to his ideas on women, free speech and worker self-determination that he was invited on a regular basis. The connection with Glasgow was put on hold, however, when he was court-martialled for refusing to fight or even drill for the 3rd London Rifles, and spent another spell of hard labour – drilling and digging – in a military compound.

After the war, Aldred moved to Glasgow permanently.

In London he had been a member of the Social Democratic Federation, but now he joined the Glasgow Anarchist Group. It was here he met Jenny Patrick, and they soon became political and personal partners. In 1935 he was impressed by Scotland's marriage laws. Caldwell quoted him saying, 'I hold that this is an institution upon which the clerics with their empty pews and their stupid English allies, have no right to speak. It is a sound, ancient institution based on common law.'

In the early years of the Russian Revolution he was a firm supporter of Lenin and the Bolsheviks, but as the Soviet State became more authoritarian, and Guy's instincts ever less so, he and the Glasgow Anarchists began to oppose it. Both the Kronstadt Rebellion, and the anarchist Emma Goldman's response to it, had a major effect on the revolutionary left worldwide. The rebellion, in 1921, was an uprising by the Baltic crews of the battleships *Petropavlovsk* and *Sevastopol* against the Soviet authorities. The sailors and their many supporters held an emergency meeting, which approved a resolution raising fifteen demands. These included immediate elections, claiming that the Soviet State no longer represented the wishes of workers and peasants, and that the elections should be secret ballots. They demanded freedom of expression for anarchists and parties left of the Communist Party, and for the right of assembly and freedom of trade unions. Under orders from Trotsky, the rebellion was put down. In her book, published soon after, Emma Goldman criticized Trotsky fiercely for his action (although he defended himself in later years, calling the Kronstadt Rebellion 'petty bourgeois').

In 1922, Aldred was still standing for election under the slogan 'Why I Am a Bolshevik'. However, by 1924 he and others had founded the Anti-Parliamentary Communist Federation (A-PCF). He would never again believe in the ability or desire of elected bodies to protect and advance the cause of working people.

Ethel Macdonald, years later in Spain, would state the anti-parliamentary case bluntly: 'There is no doubt that the magnificent struggle of the Spanish workers challenges the entire theory and historical interpretation of parliamentary socialism. The Civil War is a living proof of the futility and worthlessness of parliamentary democracy as a medium of social change. It clearly demonstrates that there is but one way, the way of direct action. And that but one class can make the change – the working class.'

Aldred, however, realised that parliaments could be used as a tool – for publicity purposes if nothing else – for radical change, and left his own A-PCF in 1932.

Fenner Brockway, an ILP member, and a man who would have crucial significance in Ethel Macdonald's life, stood for Parliament, saying, 'Let us form a united movement and use Parliament only as a sounding-board for the workers' demands.' Guy decided that this was the right way forward and, in 1934, formed his anarcho-socialist United Socialist Movement (USM). From then on until his death in 1964 he regularly put himself and the USM forward for election, claiming, as Sinn Féin would later do, that if elected he would refuse to attend the House.

*May no worldly ambition,*
*No temptation in this wilderness of understanding,*

*Lead me to serve the enemy of man,*
*The principle of power and domination.*

(from 'Meditation', by Guy Aldred)

~

Guy Aldred was a confirmed socialist-anarchist, a man not comfortable with any party line – described as 'divisive' by some – when Ethel met him, and joined the USM in the early 1930s. Aldred was living then with Jenny Patrick in Baliol Street in Glasgow; he and Rose Witcop had drifted apart, although they remained close comrades until her death in 1932.

Ethel had returned from London to Glasgow in her usual way – unannounced. She always kept close enough to her family, but was not good at letting them know in advance of her plans. Her sister Carrie, who had been a schoolgirl when Ethel left, was working now, in Lewis's in Glasgow. One day, a neatly dressed woman in her mid twenties walked up to her counter and said: 'Do you know who I am?'

''Course I do,' Carrie replied. 'My sister. Ethel.'

At least one of her brothers, Gordon, and possibly Ian too, had met with Ethel while she was in London. No letters from her from that time survive, but she knew where Carrie worked and decided to go and see her there.

'She wanted to know what the situation was at home,' Freddie explained to me. 'She was testing the water about going home. Carrie told her she should just go and speak to their mum.'

It seems mother and itinerant daughter made up, at least enough for Ethel to go back to live at 133 Calder Road. She would not be there for long.

In the months just prior to her return, Guy had opened an advice bureau for workers in the centre of Glasgow, advertising 'Legal Advice. Letters Written. Typing done.' According to John Taylor Caldwell, 'It was a miserable little office with a table, one chair, no lighting, no toilet . . . Mostly Guy was rewarded with a shilling. Which was as much as could be expected from his poverty-stricken customers.'

There are three stories about when Ethel met Guy. The first one we already know: they met when she first went to Glasgow, after losing her baby. The second theory is they met once she got to London, in the mid 1920s. In that scenario, both were speaking at a rally in Hyde Park; Guy learned that Ethel had nowhere to stay so he quickly found somewhere for her. Caldwell, and other political friends of them both, however, claim that their first meeting was when Ethel came to the Queen Street advice centre as a customer. In London, Ethel was not well known enough yet, or politically fluent enough to speak.

Looking for work back in Scotland after her debacle with Lyons' Corner Houses she went to the employment bureau. They told her there was a vacancy for a post in Dumfries. The family believe it was either a chambermaid's or waitress's position in a hotel, or perhaps in service with a rich family. Ethel had a good chance of getting it, having already had experience in hotels in the Highlands, and her work in with Lyons – as long, of course, as she did not tell them how that employment ended. Having no money, she did what she always did – travelled there through a mixture of walking, hitching and taking the odd cheap local bus. Arriving at the employers she was told that the post had already been taken.

She had made a 150-mile round trip, mainly on foot, in the middle of winter, for nothing. Ethel was understandably not best pleased, and decided to take action against 'the Buroo'.

'Early in 1933,' Ethel wrote later, 'the Labour exchange sent me after a job as a waitress at Dumfries, but when I arrived I found the whole thing was a fake, and I had to hitchhike back to Glasgow. I went to see a well-known Socialist (Guy Aldred) to ask him to fight my case. He invited me to act as his secretary.'

She would not have stepped into Aldred's office by chance. No one in Glasgow involved in politics in the 1930s was unaware of 'the Guy They All Dread' – 'they', of course, being MPs, employers, and all those involved in Church and State. Whether or not she had already met Guy in London, being on the left of politics in Glasgow she would know who he was.

The story goes that when Ethel came into the centre she barely got round to presenting her own employment complaint to either Guy or Jenny. They had a bigger problem on their hands. One of Guy's clients worked for an office supplies company. There was a deal around at the time which allowed prospective clients free three-month trials of equipment. For years to come, the advice centre and the USM would take up the offer use the typewriters and stencil duplicators to create and mass-produce their papers and leaflets. Then, when the three months were up, they sent the machines back, and started on another 'free trial'. In 1933 they had one such duplicator but only an old pre-war typewriter. Neither Guy nor Jenny could use the machines, nor knew how to type. Ethel, it is said, looked at the typewriter, stated, 'It can't be that hard,' and sat down to type. Despite all the words she was to write over the next 25 years, she never became proficient, using only two fingers on each hand. Even so, she was better than Guy or Jenny. Ethel was appointed secretary first to the A–PCF and then to the USM.

It is worth putting the USM and A–PCF in perspective. The major political and working-class parties at the time were the Labour Party, the Independent Labour Party and the Communist Party. Anarchist-leaning activists were few, but far from insignificant. In the early 1930s socialist ideas were still in flux, more than they are today. The events, objectives and interpretations that had people moving between parties were still new and very hot. The Russian Revolution was only a little over a decade old – people were still watching, assessing its development and reacting, and developments came thick and fast from Moscow.

After the revolution, the socialist and, to a lesser extent, anarchist organisations divided their loyalties between the Bolsheviks and the social democrats. Anarchism, with its emphasis on working-class organisation, tended at first to sympathise with the Bolsheviks. The turning point, however, came with the Kronstadt rising in 1921 and the Soviet government's attacks on peasant anarchist leaders in Georgia. In 1922 Aldred would still describe himself as a Bolshevik; by the end of the decade, when the realities of Stalinism were beginning to be known, he most certainly would not.

Leon Trotsky was deported from the Soviet Union in 1929, and was now actively writing and critiquing from abroad. Aldred, Ethel and Jenny were not classic Trotskyists, but they supported wholeheartedly his criticisms of the Soviet Union.

Ramsay MacDonald had brought the Labour Party into a National Government in 1931, dividing socialist opinion drastically. When Ethel began work in Queen Street that government was still in power.

In the world of the late twenties and mid thirties, after the stock market crashes and unemployment reaching colossal levels, it is no wonder, given the pace of events, that parties, groups and movements not only sprung up and disbanded, but changed direction internally. When we talk of Jenny Patrick, or Ethel, being 'anarchist', we must bear in mind that the very term was fluid. Undoubtedly Jenny, in the years immediately before the Spanish Civil War, was closer to the Glasgow Anarchist Group, which a decade before Guy himself had helped form. As for Ethel, her heart and mind were, put simply, left of Soviet communism. She distrusted politburos as much as parliaments, and worked for a grassroots, anti-authoritarian, genuinely democratic future. We will look at anarchism itself in closer detail when Ethel's journey takes us to Catalonia but, from all her writings, it is clear that she supported the idea of organised proletarian and peasant revolution – an idea that anarchists would pursue passionately.

～

The meeting of Glasgow Anarchists Jenny Patrick had called to secure support for her visit to Spain had not gone well. Far from contributing financially to the mission, as she had hoped, they did not even back the project. Old divisions came to the fore and a row developed between Jenny and the rest of the members.

The Glasgow Quartet of Guy, Ethel, John and Jenny would undoubtedly have met too regarding the invitation to Barcelona – they regularly gathered in the evenings for discussions anyway, and people of different political hues would join them for those open debates. 'Guy would speak, for instance, on the history of the tool, that if it hadn't been for the development of technology how could mankind have progressed. That sort of thing. I remember speaking about Christianity in the first four centuries,' recalled Caldwell.

'Ethel was very dominant at these discussions. I didn't talk too much because the others were such powerful personalities. Guy knew much more about Christianity than I did. He'd been a boy preacher and was terribly well up on theology.'

That night after Jenny's fall-out with the Glasgow Anarchists, however, they would have met alone. Jenny reported that the Group was annoyed that Prudhommeaux's letter had come to Guy instead of to them. Guy was becoming an internationally renowned figure – some suspected through his own 'cultivation of the personality', a Stalinist idea totally abhorrent to them. None of the Glasgow Anarchists in attendance had been amenable to the notion of using their limited funds to send Jenny to Spain. Many refused even to support the idea that anyone should go to Barcelona.

Ramsay Macdonald's National Government of 1931 had forced the split between Aldred and the A-PCF. Labour's decision to join forces with Conservatives and Liberals was seen as the most contemptuous of moves, vindicating every-thing anti-parliamentarians had believed about democratic politics. According to Caldwell, Aldred finally made his decision to leave the A-PCF in February 1933. 'The betrayal of MacDonald and the general collapse of the Labour Party ... made it so clear to the workers that Parliament was not the way to Socialism that Anti-Parliamentary propaganda seemed superfluous . . . It was no longer necessary to pioneer Anti-Parliamentarism, because Parliamentarism has collapsed.'

'Now let us preach *socialism*,' Aldred announced. If MPs could be so cynical, then Aldred would be cynical too – he would use Parliament, not to further his own career, but to expound his causes. He formed the United Socialist Movement to make use of the ballot box. For the next 30 years Aldred presented himself for election, using the machinery of liberal democracy to broadcast his views. The A-PCF were utterly opposed to this tactic.

Jenny, not only at that day's meeting, but previously and again in months to come, tried to heal the divisions between the A-PCF and the USM. It seemed she failed. One response of the Anti-Parliamentarians could not be clearer: 'You express the desire for unity between the USM and the A-PCF. You might as well desire unity between the Roman Catholic Church and the Free Thought movement . . . The A-PCF believes in and practises members' democracy . . . The USM, on the contrary, is in practice a congregation with Guy Aldred as high priest, the members follow like sheep, accepting his authority without question.'

Aldred did not accept such a charge. The differences

between the two groups were ideological, nothing to do with his leadership. As for the invitation to Barcelona, he argued it was he and the USM who had been in correspondence with the French anarchists for many years.

The four friends reconvened in Ethel's flat at 23 Gibson Street and discussed what to do about Prudhommeaux's invitation. There were two problems – who should go to Barcelona, and how could the trip be paid for? The second was hardly worth discussing, especially now that the Anarchist Group had decided not to contribute. There were simply no funds available for such a project. If they sent anyone at all, they would just have to fundraise what they could. They all agreed it was a wonderful opportunity. Something of the utmost importance was happening and it was essential that they understood it, that they help in any way they could, and that they brought back ideas and news, untainted by the privately owned media, to the working people of the UK.

At the time, Guy and Jenny had a tiny place in 'a one-room decaying tenement in Baliol Street near Charing Cross' as Caldwell described it. When Ethel Macdonald had joined Guy Aldred as a full-time worker, according to Caldwell, she was living in Cathcart Road. There is no record of when Ethel decided to leave the family home in Calder Road, Bellshill, for the flat in Cathcart. Presumably she stayed at home just long enough to catch her breath after her eventful London life, and find a flat she could afford.

'Cathcart is some distance from the centre of Glasgow,' Caldwell points out. 'This was inconvenient. It was obviously better if they lived near each other . . . [Guy] rented Ethel a top flat in Gibson Street, half a mile away. The rent and rates were £8 per quarter. The idea was to have a girl lodger to share the expense.' But the plan never worked out.

Ethel lived in that third-floor flat until her death – except for the crucial year between November 1936 and November 1937. But who else lived there? It is often said that all four comrades lived together. Caldwell, though, states that Guy and Jenny kept on the Baliol Street flat, and indeed, that was where Guy died, many years later. Gibson Street became the friends' headquarters; Caldwell moved in just after Ethel, and both Guy and Jenny were there a lot, staying over regularly.

Gibson Street is a nexus point in Glasgow. In the 1930s it stood at the edge of the city's very traditional middle-class area but in the heart of the student campus, as it does to this day, though the university was much less liberal then than now. Less salubrious housing lies behind it, and the city centre itself is just up the road beginning at Charing Cross. People would not only have wondered, given the inhabitants of 23 Gibson Street's politics, about their personal sleeping arrangements, but will have twitched their curtains, gossiped at shops. 'The neighbours were all shocked,' Caldy laughed, at his living unmarried with a woman. 'They called me Mr MacDonald, pretending they thought I was Ethel's brother. The butcher opposite would serve me, but the look of disapproval!'

Of Ethel's love life Freddie Turrell told me, 'It was never talked about in the family. I never thought about the situation between the four of them when I went visiting with my mum. It was only later I got to thinking.'

Caldwell has spoken about their lives together, but has said different things at different times over his long life. In his interview with Alison Murphy, when he was 94 years old, he said that Guy and Jenny were a couple, and he and Ethel close friends – 'We were separate individuals who sometimes had it off a wee bit.' Beyond the confines of the flat, Guy and Jenny acted like a couple. 'When Ethel and I were in public we were completely separate. Sex had nothing to do with other people. Ethel believed that I could have as many "friends" as I liked, and she could too. We had separate rooms.'

We know now, of course, about teenage Ethel's passionate love affair a decade earlier with the American merchant seaman, which perhaps helps to explain why Ethel's approach to relationships from then on was not straightforward.

The idea that all four were sexually freer together than Caldwell claimed at the end of his life has persisted, amongst family, friends and colleagues, perhaps because it is appealing to think that these four radicals flaunted social mores and lived as a *ménage à quatre*, a kind of mini Glaswegian Bloomsbury group, in the midst of morally staid pre-war Glasgow. (It is likely, in fact, that the two groups were aware of each other through mutual friends like John Maynard Keynes). But all this speculation is of no importance whatsoever. Whatever their relationships, discussion of sexuality and partners would have got in the way of their real purpose in life: social change. In 1936, with Hitler in Berlin, Mussolini in Rome, and the Spanish generals about to launch an attack on a dearly won republic, there were other more important things to do, talk about and write about. Not only that, but Aldred stood regularly for Parliament during the years the Quartet lived together: his politics alone drew abuse and hatred from the press, churches and most of the political class. Public knowledge of irregular domestic arrangements would have been counter-productive – even to his natural supporters. The West of Scotland working class in the 1930s was largely morally conservative.

What *does* matter is that they worked as a group – not only the four of them, but all their comrades in the USM and other organisations. That night, having to take a decision on Spain, only the political and practical questions would have been addressed.

'Why don't we both go?'

Perhaps Ethel put the question, when the decision came down to sending either herself or Jenny to Barcelona. But Prudhommeaux couldn't even afford to bring *one* person over. Nor could the USM.

'Then the problem is hardly made any bigger by sending two.'

According to Caldwell, one of the reasons Guy was keener that Ethel should go was age. Ethel was 27 years old, whereas Jenny was 'a couple of years older than Guy' – in her mid fifties. He wanted a young representative from Scotland to show that radicalism was alive and well and not the preserve of an older generation. It is also possible that, if indeed he and Jenny were exclusive partners, he preferred to have her at his side.

As for Ethel, she would have liked to have Jenny's company. Not that she was scared of travelling alone – all her life she had ventured out, most of the time, by herself. As a writer, she needed to be happy with her own company, and alone she could observe people better. But it was a long journey, however they made it, and she had never been out of the English-speaking world before. Jenny would be good company and had contacts, friends of friends, even in Barcelona: when you belong to a movement, the world shrinks.

The USM barely had the price of a single ticket to Carlisle.

'There are anarchists and radicals everywhere. We can fundraise as we go along.'

The plan was practical – or at least as practical as two impoverished political women could hope for, and it reflected the way Ethel had always lived, step by step, penniless, with nowhere to stay. Another walk, another hitchhike. She had done it at 16 going north to work in the Highlands, made the lonely journey home again, gone off again, still not 20 years old, to London, 400 miles away. She had had walked half the country in search of work and money, and spent long days in the rain selling papers. She was ready for another hard journey into an unclear future.

# 4

# Banderas Rojas – y Negras

> ∿ What have we in Spain? The common people
> struggling for their liberty. A struggle is taking place
> in Spain that should have the assistance of all decent-
> minded men and women in every part of the world. ∿

On 20 October 1936 Ethel Macdonald and Jenny Patrick set
out for Barcelona. As Prudhommeaux had made the official
invitation on behalf of the anarchist CNT (the National
Anarchist Union) and the FAI (Iberian Anarchist Federation),
Ethel was his named representative. Jenny's position was less
clear: she went as a voluntary delegate from the Scottish
anarchist movement.

Jenny's involvement, however, boosted funds for their
travel, despite her having fallen out with the Glasgow
Anarchist Group. She was the better known of the two
women and attracted more donations. Even with that extra
input, however, there was only enough money to send
them as far as London. There they met with radicals and
revolutionaries who gave them lodgings and helped them

raise the fare for the next stage of their journey. Several meetings were held in Hyde Park until enough had been made to get them to Paris. Ethel and Jenny were in a hurry. It is possible that, had they stayed longer, they could have raised all the finance needed. But events were racing ahead in Catalonia. The sooner they got there, the better.

According to Freddie Turrell, his aunt never told her family she was going to Spain. There was some considerable hostility in that period between Ethel and her family, her mother in particular. Daisy, that very 'Victorian' lady, had had a lot to thole in recent years. Her daughter, instead of continuing with her education, and despite her abilities, had gone off to tend bar in a hotel. On her return she had been pregnant by a married, and absent, lover. After the miscarriage, the restless girl had gone off to London. When she returned she had made friends and set up home with a group of people Daisy did not approve of.

Daisy was progressive in her own way and, though religious, Spiritualism was hardly old-time restrictive Protestantism. But Guy Aldred was still too much for her. His well-publicised views on marriage, free love and the rights of women and workers were very different from Daisy's, and doubtlessly Andrew's too. Guy was never known for his personal tact: he was a political campaigner to his core, uninterested in social niceties. Daisy knew next to nothing about the young Northern Irishman, Caldy, who had moved in with her daughter. The rumours about Ethel's domestic arrangements must have pained and embarrassed Daisy. She will have worried, too, that Ethel was being a bad influence on her younger sister. When Carrie, still not very long out of school, went up to Glasgow, she preferred to stay at Ethel's rather than getting the last bus back to Bellshill. Apart from those visits there was little communication between Ethel and the rest of her family. The first the Macdonalds heard of Ethel having left Scotland at all was nearly ten months later when she was reported missing. Apart from the shock, the circumstances in which the family received the news caused a whole new set of problems.

Perhaps Ethel had feared that her family might have tried to stop her from going – not an unreasonable reaction, given that open war was raging in the south and northwest of Spain. The newspapers were full of reports of the indiscriminate killing of priests and nuns and the invasion and appropriation of private property. For the British press, the story was one of anarchy, not anarchism. The actual situation that Ethel was about to find herself in was very different.

If Ethel ever wrote in more detail about her journey to France from London, her words have been lost. We only know of the difficult, if impressively speedy, trek to Barcelona from John Taylor Caldwell's memories of conversations with her when she returned. But, many years later, Ethel and Guy Aldred donated all their papers relating to the Barcelona visit to the Mitchell Library in Glasgow. From them we can guess at the dates they passed through Paris and arrived in Barcelona. The first newspaper in that collection is *Le Combat Syndicaliste*. The headline on Friday 1 October 1936 is 'L'U.R.S.S. et la CNT – Une Position Inadmisable'. And they were in Barcelona by the end of the month – the newspaper headline in *Tierra Y Libertad* for Saturday 23

October reads 'Galicia Under Fascist Terror!' Three weeks at most to make the thousand-mile journey by trains, boat, buses, cars, and on foot, including the stops to raise funds.

In Paris she and Jenny repeated the same operation as in London: they stayed with comrades and spoke at rallies and meetings. Again, they delayed only long enough to find the price of two train tickets halfway to Perpignan on the Spanish border. All their funds spent, they had to walk and hitchhike the last section of the journey. Farmers and country folk, few of them doubtlessly having anything to do with anarchism or the Spanish war, gave them food, lifts and a bed for the night out of common decency.

According to Caldwell, André Prudhommeaux was waiting for them in Perpignan. After a day or two of rest, he accompanied them across the border. Once in Spain, Prudhommeaux handed Ethel and Jenny over to the care of Augustin Souchy. Souchy was a German anarchist and journalist who had been a close comrade of Pyotr Kropotkin, the foremost advocate of anarchist communism until his death. During World War I, Souchy had fled Germany for Sweden to avoid conscription. But the Swedish government expelled him in 1917 for his radical anti-militarist activities. Since then he had been a frequent visitor to Spain and a friend of the Spanish left. He was also active within the CNT. Souchy took Ethel and Jenny to Barcelona, introducing them to the people with whom they would be working, and who would find them lodgings. Jenny Patrick logged their jubilant arrival in her diary:

Tuesday, 3 November was the most exciting day in both of our lives and I don't think we'll ever forget it. We handed in our papers and after they realised we were comrades, they were terribly nice to us. They asked us if we had money and we told them the truth that we were broke. They took us to a restaurant and we had a wonderful time. Everyone was bright and cheerful and happy. So naturally we were the same. We felt full of enthusiasm. This was revolution.

In that edition of *Tierra y Libertad* the abstract of the leading article addressed the unpredictable real-world situation into which Ethel had arrived: 'A situation can never be defined in any given moment, because in politics unexpected elements come into play which change the nature of this war and our Revolution.' But Ethel Macdonald's first dispatches home were not about politics – yet. Like any young woman out of her country for the first time, in a beautiful city, she wrote about Barcelona itself:

*Barcelona 8th November*

Barcelona is a marvellous place in its architecture. The buildings are really wonderful. Each one gleaming brightly and not a trace of soot or grime . . . In the main square, the Plaza de la Republica, the white walls of the Generalitat, the government offices, glisten in brilliant sunshine . . . Birds are singing in the trees and the sky is the most beautiful blue I have ever seen.

That beautiful blue sky did not greet her every day, however:

I cannot remember what I was doing on Tuesday, but I
know it was pouring cats and dogs. Sunny Spain! Sometimes, yes! But Glasgow cannot compare with Barcelona
for rain. We get wet, dry ourselves, and get wet again!

What a life! Even the work men go about with um-
brellas on the job!

Although she was in a country so very different from her
own, Ethel quickly noted echoes of her own world and the
global movement she was involved in. Back in Scotland,
The Glasgow Anarchists had their headquarters in an old
Victorian terraced house which they called Bakunin House,
an important political centre throughout, and after, the
1920s. From Barcelona, Ethel wrote: 'As regards International
House, the militia's centre here, it is called, I am told Caserna
Bakunin – Bakunin House! But Glasgow anticipated even
revolutionary, Anti-Fascist Barcelona, with its own Bakunin
House, established in 1920!'

Ethel wasted no time in sending her reports home – to
the *Bellshill Speaker*, a large and significant daily newspaper
at the time, covering the whole of industrial Lanarkshire and
the west coast. She wrote, too, for Glasgow's *Evening Times*,
and, on one occasion at least, even for the *Mail*. She continued writing for *Regeneración,* her articles either appearing
under her own name, in correspondence from Catalonia, or
providing information for Guy to write up. Amongst updates
on the Nationalist rebels' advances, the political developments in the city, and impassioned pleas for solidarity, Ethel
included little human details of everyday life in a war zone:
'Sugar is practically impossible to obtain and I have not seen

an egg since I came. Milk also is unobtainable, but I believe that this is due to the fact that it is kept for the children and sent to those of Madrid. But Tangerines! Today I got 20 for 2 pesetas! Fruit and vegetables are very cheap.' She was describing a situation that, in three years' time, when World War II broke out, all her readers would begin to experience for themselves.

The tone of her descriptions of Barcelona chimes closely with those of George Orwell, who arrived in the city a little less than two months after Ethel, in December 1936, and stayed for a similar period of time – although much of that he spent fighting at the Aragon front. He himself declared that he went to Spain not to write but to fight. Given that all non-fascist European states, apart from the Soviet Union, adopted a policy of non-intervention in the Spanish war, the only way a man could play his part against the rise of fascism was to volunteer. Orwell did so, enlisting with the help of the Independent Labour Party, which sent him to Barcelona and the POUM (United Marxist Workers Party) militia.

He wrote about his early reflections on arrival in the city in *Homage to Catalonia*:

It was the first time that I had ever been in a town where the working class was in the saddle. Practically every building of any size had been seized by the workers and was draped with red flags or the red and black flags of the Anarchists . . . Every shop had an inscription saying that it had been collectivized, even the bootblacks had been collectivized and their boxes painted red and black. Waiters and shop-walkers looked you in the face and treated you as an equal. Servile and even ceremonial forms of speech had temporarily disappeared. Nobody said 'Señor' or 'Don' or even 'usted'. Everyone called everyone else 'Comrade' and 'thou' and said 'Salud' instead of 'Buenos días'. Tipping was forbidden . . . this really was a workers' state! . . . Above all there was a belief in the revolution and the future, a feeling of having suddenly emerged into an era of equality and freedom. Human beings were trying to behave as human beings and not cogs in the capitalist machine. In the barbers' shops were Anarchist notices (the barbers were mostly Anarchists) solemnly explaining that barbers were no longer slaves. In the streets were coloured posters appealing to prostitutes to stop being prostitutes.

Later, when he was recovering in hospital from the bullet he caught in his neck, he wrote to his friend Cyril Connolly: 'I have seen wonderful things and at last really believe in Socialism, which I never did before.'

Ethel and Jenny were at first found digs in a crumbling tenement in the Barrio Gótico, not far from Las Ramblas, and closer still to the CNT–FAI headquarters. It was from here that Ethel wandered out on her first days in the city, noticing the blueness of the sky, the birds in the trees, and the anarchist militia. As their central objective was to find out more about the grassroots political situation and report how daily lives operate in a revolutionary situation, they had to surmount language barriers. This was difficult. Not only were there two local languages, Catalan and Castillian Spanish, there were also international volunteers and reporters from all over Europe. French, German and Italian were heard on the streets, and the Madrid government's pact with the Soviet Union meant that there were many Russian speakers around too. The original plan had been to move Ethel and Jenny into International House, a CNT residence, but when the plan was changed Ethel came into closer contact with the many nationalities in Barcelona – volunteers, for the most part, in the International Brigades.

'Yesterday we moved our residence, not to International House – that will be headquarters and receiving centre for militia who are resting – but to Sacha's place. Here there are Sacha, Hanka (his companion), Dori, Jenny, another comrade, a Russian I believe, and me. But daily this place is flooded with people of all nationalities. Most of them are about 25 to 30 years old. Romanians, Bulgarians, Russians, Germans . . . I like the international atmosphere . . . This is the kind of International that will unite the human race . . .'

Everyone she met was, naturally, filled with enthusiasm for the revolution, and wanted to speak of nothing else: 'Last night, Dori, Sacha, Fortin, Jenny and I met to discuss the problem of propaganda.' Settling in was a mix of excitement and simple chores, new acquaintances and hope: 'Yesterday, we removed our goods. After arranging beds, etc, we ate just good old English teas – tomatoes, cheese, etc. And when everyone is replete, they sing the international songs together . . . I get a thrill out of being here. I feel alive and full of energy.'

There was no clear lingua franca, but Spanish would obviously have been a useful language to know. By her own admission, though, Ethel never managed to master it. 'I am afraid that our knowledge of Spanish is progressing very slowly. We have arrived at the stage when we can ask for "two coffees with milk" and say "salud", so that is pretty bad!

'I hope I pick up Spanish so that I can get a thorough knowledge of the International Movement.'

But learning the language continued to be a problem: 'I had my first experience today, of trying to speak to a Spaniard. I do not know what he was talking about, and I could not be sure that he could understand what I was trying to say! Everyone says it is very simple, but to me, the pronunciation is like committing suicide. I almost choke over each word. Nothing depresses me so much as the fact that I don't understand what is being said and am unable to ask for exactly what I want. It gives me an inferiority complex.'

She tried to rectify the situation by concentrating on learning from books, but, as many students discover, text-book languages are usually very different from their street varieties: 'Lessons in speaking are one thing, and speaking to the Spanish in their own tongue is another. I daresay I will improve gradually. At least, I had better improve, and not too gradually . . . Most Britishers think the people who live in the country are the foreigners but I am very conscious of the fact that I am the stranger.'

For a writer, polemicist, and soap-box demagogue, this feeling of exclusion must have been galling. All her life Ethel had debated, argued and developed her own thinking through conversations with others. Her comments on language continued to reflect a mix of frustration and little victories: 'I labour under many disadvantages. I have met one of the comrades who spoke at the meeting I told you about.

He insists on speaking Spanish all the time in order to make me learn. I can now read the papers a little and can speak a few words, but I intend to make good progress within a short time. There is always a long period of listening and then, suddenly, you find that you understand. At least, that is how I am with French.'

'My French is progressing slowly,' she comments later. 'All languages are spoken here, but those who understand English are few and far between. We all live here together, but we have to get our food outside . . .'

In a letter they wrote to Guy, Ethel and Jenny shared their concern about how they would fit into their new world and the roles they should play: 'You know how bad things seem sometimes on first impressions and then come out alright. Anyway we intend to stick it out, if we can get anything at all to do, whether useful or not, as we don't want to return like bad pennies.'

Quite apart from the day-to-day necessity of getting by with shop assistants and stall holders, Ethel had her eye on the future: 'Don't you think it will be good for the British movement when I return, if I read and speak Spanish?'

Even speaking in English caused her problems: 'Some people here seem to imagine that the Scotch do not speak nor write English! At least, they imagine that the Scotch pronounce it with a foreign accent. The amount of people who have asked me if I can speak English! And they do not mean it unkindly. It amuses me.'

70

Dreux is a shabby town west of Paris with a high percentage of North African immigrants. It came to international attention only once in recent centuries – when France's National Front Party won elections in 1983, seizing control of the city council and deputy mayorship.

It is home now for 90-year-old Antonia Fontanillas. We sit in her tiny kitchen, in a 1940s flat that, in Scotland, would be called a single end. Her window looks onto a dilapidated swing park where children of several origins – North African, Pakistani, French, Chinese – play together amidst uncollected rubbish and broken glass.

Antonia was 19 when Ethel Macdonald and she were both in Barcelona. It is possible that the two women came across each other – their political and geographical worlds were certainly very close. 'I met a great many foreign women in those days,' she tells me. 'But I didn't always know their names, or if I did, I can't recall them now. I don't remember Ethel specifically.' Nor does Ethel mention Antonia in any of her dispatches home. But then, Antonia was neither an international volunteer, nor in any position of power. That is precisely what makes her so interesting. We have histories and memoirs of leaders and 'professional' observers of the Spanish Revolution, but precious little from the very people who made that revolution, particularly women. Antonia's account of her own personal experiences in 1936 and 1937 are invaluable, and throw light on Ethel's own life at the time.

'It was a completely different type of revolution because it emerged from people's hard work and efforts,' Antonia tells me. After the war, Antonia's family was one of the few active

71

Republican families to have stayed on in Spain. Eventually, however, circumstances became too tough. Franco had a long memory and persecuted his old enemies for the entire 40 years of his reign. Antonia had gone to France and met her husband there, but now lives alone, a widow in a foreign country.

'I was in Barcelona in 1934, but I didn't take part in any anarchist group before 1936.' She shows me photographs of a young, bright-eyed, dark-haired girl. In some of them she wears the red bandana of the anarchists. Despite the passage of 70 years, the girl in the photographs is immediately recognisable as the elderly lady sitting across the table from me now. Her hair is thinner and grey, but her smile is the same and her eyes haven't dimmed. 'I wanted to, I really wanted to be a part of it all. Instead I used to go with my father to all the political meetings. They used to meet at the bullrings, at the Monumental. Those meetings were always packed with people.'

Ethel and Antonia were, on the surface, two very different people: a Scot and a Catalan. One chose to travel to Spain to support, and report on, the revolution and the war. The other, by accident of birth, was necessarily caught up in her country's struggles. Ethel had arrived already a deeply politicised person; Antonia became politicised by circumstances. On another level, though, were they really so dissimilar? They were both working class. They had grown up in, essentially, the same free market system. They were of a generation that faced the threat of fascism – more directly in Antonia's case, although Oswald Mosley was gaining strength and power across Britain. (Just as Ethel was leaving London, in fact, the Battle of Cable Street – in which Mosley's British Union of Fascists, dressed as blackshirts and shouting anti-Semitic and racist slogans, were confronted by protesters – was taking place. Working men and women and Jewish, Irish and left-wing organisations were suddenly pulled together to challenge the threat.)

Antonia and Ethel lived at a time when women's education and the role women played in political organisations and movements were still, to say the least, undervalued. Yet both, in their own ways, alongside their sisters, played a highly active and crucial part in the events of their time. Antonia Fontanillas, not yet 20 and full of hope, energy and commitment, was the kind of local girl that Ethel would have met regularly on the streets, at the market, in meetings.

At 90 years old, Antonia still laughs a lot, and easily. Despite Franco's ultimate victory and the misery he visited on her and her family for the bulk of her life, her optimism today is a reflection of the young woman she once was. 'We supported the concept of loyalty, honesty – those are the basic values of anarchism. To sacrifice rather than profit. It is about breaking down barriers, not to be subservient, but to fight to become decent people, for our own dignity.'

'We' for Antonia was just about everyone in Catalonia at the time, and specifically those who identified themselves with anarchism, people like herself who, first and foremost, were opposed to fascism and who were dedicated to the ideal of social justice. Ethel shared with Antonia and her friends a radicalism, the same determination to take on and defeat the monarchists and the military. They also shared a suspicion of the increasingly communist-backed Republican government.

The vast majority of international volunteers to Spain were young men, but a great many women from many countries played an active part. Some, like Annie Murray, joined the Republic's medical corps. Murray, from Aberdeenshire, was already a communist as a nurse at Edinburgh's Royal Infirmary, and served in Spain throughout the entire duration of the Civil War. Thora Silverton, from Wales, was another communist nurse, who volunteered at the Aragon front. Londoner Penny Phelps nursed the wounded of the International Brigades at the Battle of Jarama until she herself was wounded and sent home in 1938.

Some women worked for the Republican cause politically, such as Katherine Stewart, the Duchess of Atholl, who visited Spain and was a vocal supporter of the Republic, both in the House of Commons and beyond. Others, like Ethel, offered support through their media work. Nancy Cunard reported on the war for the *Manchester Guardian*, while Dorothy Parker, like many other well-known writers and artists, was a dedicated campaigner for the Republic and the war against fascism; in 1937 she went to Spain and broadcast her support from Radio Madrid. 'Red Ellen' Wilkinson was a member of the ILP, the National Union of Women's Suffrage Societies, and a founder member of the Fabian Society. A history student at Manchester University as early as 1910, she became a Member of Parliament in 1923. She and Clement Atlee reported on German collaboration from Spain at the end of 1936. Returning home, she founded, with Charlotte Haldane, J.B. Priestley, Eleanor Rathbone and

Katherine Stewart, a fundraising organisation for the families of *brigadistas*.

There was also military involvement by women. Marion Merriman was an administrative officer with the American Abraham Lincoln Battalion, while Felicia Browne, an English communist, was one of many women who took up arms. Felicia left Slade Art School in 1936 and became a *milicana* on the Aragon front in July 1936 – she was tragically the first British volunteer to be killed in the Civil War.

～

In histories of the Spanish Civil War, it is striking how often the Spanish Revolution is ignored, or at best commented on only briefly in passing. The Spanish ideological battle has been seen as, fundamentally, a stand-off between monarchist Catholicism on the one side, and an alliance of communists and socialist democrats on the other. Apart from not actually explaining how the war came about, this approach gives the impression that anarchism, at its apogee in the mid 1930s in Barcelona, was a flash in the pan, a spontaneous insurrection that came from nowhere and led to nothing.

Noam Chomsky, one of anarchism's most important contemporary thinkers, agrees that this portrayal of the revolution is misleading: 'There had been decades of preparation for [the revolution]. The formation, over years, of free schools, educational programmes, collectives; efforts at establishing a real anarchist system – all of which was eventually crushed by force. There was a long preparatory period in the general population in which the ideas, assumptions, the conceptions of how to run a more free society became instilled in people. What looks spontaneous was in fact the end result of a long period of education, organisation and experimentation.'

Chomsky's analysis runs contrary to communist thought – anarchism in the early days of the Spanish Revolution was seen as 'primitive', a naïve movement which came out of repression and abuse and urgently needed shaping. The communists felt that, without the necessary discipline and organisation, an historic opportunity would be squandered. The people needed political training and guidance – and they needed it fast, with the Nationalist army making rapid progress from the Spanish south.

In the late nineteenth century, Mikhail Bakunin, Russian revolutionary and one of the founders of anarchism, saw in Spain a social and political situation where his ideas might develop. He sent an Italian comrade, Giuseppe Fanelli, to recruit members for the First International. Bakunin's and Fanelli's ideas chimed well in many parts of the country, particularly in the countryside. Spain was then, and would be for many years to come, one of the least industrially developed states in Western Europe, and thus had a high percentage of rural workers. Throughout the late nineteenth and early twentieth centuries there had been a series of rebellions in the countryside. Andalusia in the south and Catalonia in the northeast were often at the centre of these conflicts with an otherwise deeply Catholic, monarchist and traditional Spain.

In the cities the resistance to capitalism was as strong but took a different form of expression. The CNT was the anarchist union; its rival, led by the socialists, was the UGT (General Workers' Union). In the cities both competed for the working class, but in Barcelona in particular the CNT, with its emphasis on the independent self-organisation of workers – syndicalism – enjoyed the majority support.

In 1934, in the town of Oviedo, Asturias, in northern Spain, striking miners were supported by socialists, communists and anarchists alike. Their dispute began with local demands, but grew in size, success and ambition. Communists point to the incendiary success of the Asturian strike to demonstrate the effectiveness of 'educated', controlled, rebellion. In his book *Revolutionaries*, Eric Hobsbawm, the British Marxist historian, claims that while the Asturian strike sparked off the Spanish Civil War, a hundred years of anarchist activity in Catalonia had caused little more than extra police activity. The anarchist response to this view would be that the Republic itself, and the conducting of an entire war, would not have been possible without a grassroots, bottom-up radicalisation, honed over the same period of time.

In October, a general strike was called for, bringing not only a confrontation between workers and the government, backed by the police and army, but also a new voice: one of the most rousing and skilful speakers of the twentieth century, Dolores Ibarurri. 'La Pasionaria' was fifteen years older than Ethel and, like her, from a working-class family of 11 children. Unlike Ethel, however, Dolores joined the Communist Party, and worked tirelessly for that cause until her death. Whereas Ethel Macdoanld edited the revolutionary paper, *Regeneración,* Ibarurri edited *Mundo Obrero* (*Workers' World*), writing under the pseudonym La Pasionaria – the passionflower. Despite their differences, she and Ethel used their influence in their respective movements to campaign for women's rights and working conditions.

La Pasionaria was elected to the Cortes, the Spanish parliament in Madrid. On the eve of the right-wing military's attack on the Republic, she spoke on the radio, crying, '*No pasarán!*' (They shall not pass!)

In the early conflicts with government troops and police, the Asturian miners and their supporters came out on top. Their flag flew over every building, and the town of Oviedo was declared a workers' commune. Within a few days, however, a much-expanded army and police force returned. The uprising lasted 15 days and cost 1,500 lives, and was eventually beaten back by an army fortified with colonial troops from Morocco, and conscripts from Galicia and the south. The entire affair was bloody, the excesses of the government's reprisals as bad, if not worse, than the violence on the streets during the strike.

Nationally, events accelerated at the start of 1936. The government was re-elected in February of that year on the basis of the same programme that had won it power five years earlier. 'It had failed to fulfil most of its promises to bring about social change,' says Professor Mike Gonzalez of Glasgow University. 'It had promised land reform and that had got diverted and not been fully implemented. It had promised trade union rights and those rights had been driven back. It had promised secular education and limits on the power of the Church – none of that had really been carried through.'

Seeing the anger amongst the working and peasant classes, conservative Spain worried that the anarchist-led masses would take over. The government was losing control. The conspirators in the military, with their supporters in the Church and among the wealthier classes, began to prepare for a military coup, and on 18 July 1936 a group of generals announced that they were rising against the Republican government.

Every barracks in every major centre rose as part of the military rebellion, including in Barcelona, but within three hours it was defeated in that city, thanks to the high level of worker organisation, overseen mainly by the CNT. The military surrendered and the city was consequently more firmly than ever in the hands of the workers' movement.

The CNT had hundreds of thousands of members in the early 1930s. When the time came, and the military rebelled, they were capable of mass mobilisation. They took whatever arms they could, built barricades, and prepared for further fascist attacks. The generals were making rapid progress in other parts of Spain, and every day they got nearer to Catalonia. The provinces of Cadiz and Seville fell almost immediately. So, too, did a vast swathe of land from Galicia in the northwest to Aragon in northern central Spain. Andalusia's proximity to Morocco meant that they suffered the full first rush of colonial troops commanded by the young rising star of the right-wing Falange, General Francisco Franco. By October the two regions were connected by a fascist-ruled corridor running through Cordoba and Toledo. The Spain which Ethel Macdonald was working in and writing about in late 1936 was roughly divided in half. The Republic controlled the centre-east, from Madrid as far south as Malaga. The Basque Country and Asturias were holding out, as was of course Catalonia and Valencia. But fighting was not far away. Navarra and most of Aragon had fallen, dividing the Catalan Republicans from their allies in Madrid and the Basque Country.

In the days just before, and during the Civil War itself, there were attacks on private property, requisitioning land for collectivisation. Most famously, there were burnings of churches, monasteries and convents, and the murder of nuns and priests. The actual figures of deaths among the clergy vary wildly, often depending on the ideological standpoint of the reporter. But there were certainly more than 6,000 victims.

I asked Noam Chomsky about this. 'Yes, at the early stages of the Spanish anarchist revolution there were acts of violence – the killing of priests, burning down churches and so on – which were unconscionable. But they were a reaction of a very oppressed people to highly oppressive institutions which had been crushing them for centuries. And when people liberate themselves unpleasant things happen.'

The attacks on Catholic clergy have become known as 'the Red Terror', but two key factors must be borne in mind. First, the Catholic Church was no innocent bystander caught in the crossfire. It was at the time a thoroughly politicised institution. Its opposition to the Republic and its profound conservatism were not only cultural and historical. The Church was also a highly active player on the Spanish right. The CEDA (the Spanish Confederation of the Autonomous Right, a party formed in 1933 by the ultra-conservative Gil Robles) was allied to the Falange. The Church hierarchy had actively campaigned against all reform for decades. And, when the attack on the Republic finally came, not only did it support the generals, but its members, including priests, took up arms and fought. There are first-hand accounts of this, for example from Jack Shaw, who joined the International Brigades at the age of 18 after a period of imprisonment following the Battle of Cable Street (he was accused of 'hitting a police inspector with a brick'). At Brunete, he recalled in an article published in the *Guardian* in 2000, 'There was a priest in the church steeple firing at us, and when he came down he pushed the villagers to shield him while he kept shooting. One of the men from the American battalion shot him dead.'

The other complication of the Church's role in Spanish politics is that not all priests, nuns and churchgoers were always against the Republic. Many Catholics across Spain were active supporters of reform, nowhere more so than in the Basque Country. There, the Church had long been separatist and saw the war against the military and monarchists as an opportunity for Basque freedom. In other words, priests and confirmed Catholics took up arms on both sides of the struggle. For General Franco, Basque and Republican priests were worse than communists or anarchists. When, in 2007, Pope Benedict XVI beatified 500 priests killed in the war, he chose only those killed by the left. His action caused outrage in Spain, particularly in the Basque Country. No clergy were honoured for their fight against fascism.

Finally, it should be remembered that the enemies of anarchists, socialists and radicals understood the negative reaction to anti-clerical violence. They often exaggerated the extent of that violence, and have even been charged with killing priests themselves to provoke domestic and international condemnation of the revolutionaries. 'So, condemn the acts, yes,' Chomsky told me, 'But understand them.'

~

Just as the rebel generals fought on behalf of a mixed bag of creeds and political interests – land and factory owners, traditionalist Catholics, right-wing conservatives, monarchists and outright Nazi-supporting fascists – the forces defending the Republic were a fusion of progressive ideologies. Chief amongst them, and at the heart of Ethel Macdonald's argument, and her fate, were anarchists, communists and Trotskyists.

The communists numerically, particularly in Catalonia, were so small as to be almost insignificant in the years leading up to the war. However, when the Republic, pushed back by the generals, desperately defending Madrid and Barcelona, turned to the Soviet Union for help, communist influence, finance and arms became of central importance.

According to Professor Mike Gonzalez, 'At the start of the war the Communist Party probably had 3,000 members or so, compared with the hundreds of thousands who were in one way or another led, or influenced, by the anarchists. They were small but, because of their connection with Russia, they had a weight, an influence, greater than their number. They offered their support to the Republican government and in doing so were really deploying the promise of Russian support. They were well organised, highly disciplined, had external support and very quickly became politically authoritative within the Republican government.'

Communists generally felt they had to look beyond the specifics of the Spanish struggle, seeing it as part of a longer process. In their eyes, a response to the rise of fascism internationally had to be played strategically. Allies had to be kept on board – France, Britain and the United States in particular. Knowing that these countries had commercial interests in Spain, the USSR deduced that a revolution in Spain would not be tolerated. Communists felt that the anarchists were being irresponsible. Pushing the Republic too far to the left would risk losing European – and Soviet – support.

Anarchists, for their part, emphasised the blatant fact that that neither France nor Britain was lending any kind of meaningful support anyway. Nazi Germany was already giving arms, planes and manpower to the generals, and Italy's contribution was even more significant. No such offer was being made by the democratic nations. Further, France and Britain made it illegal even for volunteers to travel to Spain and fight in the anti-fascist cause. *Brigadistas* had to be, in effect, smuggled out of the country, or pretend to be travelling for personal or business reasons. To many leftists in Spain this was not just part of the European appeasement programme, but outright opposition to, and fear of, the revolution.

For the rank-and-file soldier or militia man who either chose to fight under the hammer and sickle or ended up doing so due to local circumstances, the macropolitical argument was generally of less importance. Professor Willy Maley's father, James, was one of the men who volunteered and went illegally to Spain to fight fascism.

'I think they were a very mixed bunch, the people who

went to fight'. Willy says 'You are talking about somebody, for instance, who went to Eton, was a well-known writer, and then someone from the Calton, working-class Glasgow, like my father. There were anarchists and communists. There were communists who weren't in the Communist Party. Different people with different kinds of radicalism. What they all had in common was their opposition to Franco.

'My father was a member of the Communist Party and he went to Spain to fight Franco and because he saw the war as a dress rehearsal for a greater struggle. Even the members of the Communist Party who went from Glasgow, from Fife and Lanarkshire didn't all see eye to eye. It wasn't all black and white.'

A little over half of the Scots *brigadistas* were members of the Communist Party, according to Daniel Gray in *Homage to Caledonia*. 'A fifth of volunteers spread their allegiances between the Labour Party and the ILP. A further fifth had no formal allegiance of membership.'

But for Ethel, the communists used Spain *only* as a pawn in a much bigger game. The people who were risking their lives in Barcelona and elsewhere were dispensable in the name of an international political game, whose ultimate aim, in anarchist eyes, was to ensure Russian power in Europe.

Jenny Patrick was a member of Guy Aldred's Anti-Parliamentarian Communist Federation; all four of the Glasgow Quartet were sympathisers with the libertarian and communist instincts of their Catalan comrades. The A-PCF had argued since the mid 1920s that Russia could not be described as a 'workers' state' at all. It simply had a new ruling class. 'To pretend that Russian Capitalism is some kind of Socialism is ridiculous,' Aldred wrote. 'We have in Russia today a propertyless class of wage earners . . . Fundamentally, it is a capitalist country.'

For Aldred and Ethel, the Soviet Union had betrayed revolutionary principles and now, in 1936, was betraying the Spanish people. They also thought that the Communist Party was mistaken about the central issue of discipline and authority. Attitude towards discipline was one of the ideological differences that had divided Marx and Bakunin at the First International in 1864. Since then, and with the success of the Russian Revolution, the principle of disciplined resistance had become holy creed for communists. Only through controlled organisation could socialism stand a chance against the wealth and power of capitalism.

The very idea of top-down discipline has always been problematic for, at least some, anarchists. However, the successes of the revolution belie the myth that anarchism is incapable of order, lawfulness and regularity. The trains did, in fact, run on time. In 1936 collectivised farms ran efficiently – in some cases more efficiently than they had done under their private owners. Military defence was generally well organised by workers' committees. Shops and businesses remained open, and prospered under a complete turnaround in management power. There were the same taxis, buses and services as there had been before. And then there were the new schools, colleges, women's education initiatives and military training provisions.

'Anarchism is not a doctrine,' says Noam Chomsky. 'Nobody laid down the dogma. Nobody has the *right* to lay down dogmas for others. I think it should best be looked at as a kind of a tendency in human thought and human action and human affairs; a tendency which is, certainly, based on principles. A fundamental principle is that authority is not self-legitimating.'

'There are a lot of misconceptions about anarchism,' echoes Mike Gonzalez. 'I suppose the standard image is somebody with a floppy hat, a large cloak and either a violin case or a smoking bomb hidden behind the cape! It's a music-hall caricature. That's not what anarchism is.

'Anarchism in Spain is a movement which grew up in two places, and with two faces. In the south of Spain they organise and mobilise poor agricultural workers against the big landowners. In Catalonia the main power, the major influence of the anarchist, is through the trade union, the CNT. It is called anarcho-syndicalism, because it lays particular emphasis on trade union organisation, but with a proviso that union organisation is built on the rank and file, the grassroots.'

In an article in the *New Statesman* in November 1936, Cyril Connolly explained why he felt that the Spanish situation clarified for him what anarchism was, seeing Spanish anarchism as a movement that had gone through three stages:

> The first was the conception of pure anarchy which grew out of the writings of Rousseau, Proudhon, Godwin, and to a lesser extent, Diderot and Tolstoy. The essence of this anarchist faith is that there exists in mankind a natural trend towards nobility and dignity; human relations based on a love of liberty combined with a desire to help each other (as shown for instance

in the mutual generosity of the poor in slum districts in cases of sickness and distress) should in themselves be enough, given education and the right economic conditions, to provide a working basis for people to live on; State interference, armies, property, would be as superfluous as they were to the early Christians.

The impediments to this ideal are the desire to gain money and power. '[If] these instincts are allowed free run there will always be war, tyranny, and exploitation. Power and money must therefore be abolished altogether.'

Connolly goes on to describe the 'second stage of Anarchism', in which he agrees with Bakunin, that the only way to abolish money and power is by 'direct action on the bourgeoisie in whom these instincts were incurably ingrained'. Finally, Connolly saw Spanish anarchism as having moved into a third phase: '[in] looking round for a suitable machinery to replace State centralisation it found syndicalism, to which it is now united. . . . The ideal of the CNT and the FAI is libertarian Communism, a Spain in which the work and wealth is shared by all.'

In addition to anarchism and communism, there was a third important movement in the Spanish struggle against fascism: Trotskyism. Leon Trotsky, one of the most important revolutionaries in Russia in 1917 had come to see the development of the Soviet Union as 'degenerated'. Power, he said, had merely been transferred from the proletariat to the party which, under Joseph Stalin, had taken an ever more totalitarian form. Socialism needed to constantly renew itself in a process of 'Permanent Revolution', an idea Marx himself had espoused. Moreover, Stalin's idea of 'socialism in one country' was anathema to Trotsky – although, again, Marx himself had declared that socialism could only function properly on a global basis. Trotskyists have as the cornerstone of their philosophy the idea that the enduring success of socialism could only be achieved on a worldwide basis.

For socialism to exist internationally, states which had not achieved advanced capitalism would have to be capable of revolution, and thereafter sustain it. Soviet communists felt that this was impossible. They also felt that the combination of two objectives – permanent *and* worldwide revolution – was a misinterpretation of Marx and Engels. Trotskyists, however, understood this as Marxism untainted by the particular desires and ambitions of the Soviet state and its Politburo. So although Troskyists had many profound problems with the anarchists, they still had enough in common to work and fight alongside them. Both saw themselves as movements absolutely tied to the grassroots, to workers and peasants. Community-based political activity was critical to both.

'Guy Aldred,' Mike Gonzalez points out, 'was emphatic that, given too much power, trade union leaders always betray their members. The only guarantee of a genuinely democratic unionism is that it is controlled entirely by the rank and file.' This was more or less the situation in Barcelona in 1936. The Spanish Republic, which was becoming every day more and more under the control of the communists, regarded anarcho-syndicalism as a danger to their vision of Spanish society and to the defence against the fascists. Consequently, anarchists and Trotskyists felt closer than ever to each other.

At this point in her life, Ethel Macdonald seldom called herself an anarchist; in truth, her politics were somewhere between anarchism and Trotskyism, and although she moved almost exclusively in anarchist circles in Barcelona, she would have had no problem with either the presence, or the aims of, for example, the POUM, which organised its own Trotskyist militia.

The distinction should be made between the leaders and thinkers of all three parts of the Republican alliance – which was already beginning to disintegrate at the end of 1936 – and the workers, peasantry, the militia men and women. The POUM fought alongside anarchist militia without many problems; in the early days both also fought side by side with communists. Antonia Fontanillas, remembering back to that time and those divisions, told me, 'There were never any problems in the factory where I used to work. I never felt there was ever a difficulty in the committee because members were of one organisation or the other.'

Willy Maley concurs. 'The interesting thing is, I never heard my father say anything about, you know, judging whether anarchists, POUM, the socialists, and so on, were right or wrong.'

Ethel Macdonald, however, was deeply concerned at the time with who was right and who was wrong – as were intellectuals on the communist side who continued to believe that the anarchist revolution in Catalonia was a distraction from the bigger struggle, nationally and inter-nationally. But the anarchists were Ethel's natural allies, and their cause was the one she felt was truly worth fighting, and dying, for.

'So, who's an anarchist?' asks Noam Chomsky. 'Well, women seeking women's rights, working people seeking workers' rights, people wanting to eliminate state structures because they're dominant, and so on. All of these are manifestations of anarchism. It's an unquenchable spirit that is pursued in different ways at different times.'

# 5

# The Revolutionary Life

*~ From out of the fields of Andalusia and Asturias, fertilised by blood of the heroic proletariat, will rise a new Spain of the proletariat. The Spain of Free Socialism! ~*

*Barcelona 1st December 1936*

Truly I should feel cheated if I were compelled to leave Spain with nothing attempted and nothing done . . . I feel that my future depends on making good here. And if, at present, I am doing less than I yearn to do for the movement, at least I am acclimatised.

By the turn of the year, Ethel would be much more involved in the movement than she could have expected.

Ethel Macdonald was no theorist. She argued and debated and understood the various forces at work in Spain. She was never happier than when surrounded by political people, discussing justice and equality. But the detail of method she left to Guy Aldred and, when in Spain, to Jenny Patrick. Guy was a feverish theorist: pro- and then anti-communist;

aligned, then non-aligned with the Trotskyists; then aligned and non-aligned again – and that in the 1930s alone! Jenny Patrick also wrote articles in Spain, and they tended to be more carefully reasoned in their ideology than Ethel's. From everyone I have spoken to who knew Ethel herself, or who knows her work and her politics, it is clear that she was an instinctive rebel. She recognised her political home when it presented itself: radical, grassroots, impatient with parliaments, anti-authoritarian. Although there is no record of them ever meeting, it seems she and George Orwell might have got on very well, despite the differences in their backgrounds.

When Ethel did try to theorise she often didn't carry it off very well: 'Spain is the key country of the world struggle today,' she wrote from Barcelona. 'But I do not see how the workers must permit the Spanish situation to urge them onto a policy of war . . . I feel that it is a dangerous idea to propagate and may tend to aid Imperialism and reaction . . .' She became somewhat inarticulate when talking in the abstract. 'One cannot support Capitalist war policy and one cannot just mark time at pacifism . . . There is only one way of developing peace: to urge against war and national armies, the workers' militia liquidating itself in industry and social [sic]. If one urges against war and Fascism the workers' militia – good!'

It is hard to know what Ethel meant. If she was arguing that Spanish workers should down weapons and up tools – concentrate solely on the revolution and ignore the war – then she was playing directly into communist suspicion and criticism that the anarchists were more concerned with their own, local, revolution than with the threat and might of fascism. If, on the other hand, she was thinking of the looming war against Hitler and Mussolini, her pacifist stance still did not reflect the broad opinion of anarchists.

But when she talks about *people*, about the realities of the situation around her, her passion and commitment shine through:

> The lights went out throughout the city. From the tops of the buildings, huge beams played across the sky, searching, searching . . . Fifteen minutes later [Jenny and I] went out. All the subways have display notices advising the people to take shelter. Hurrying to and fro were the militia, armed. It was marvellous! . . . I was told that on one occasion, at the beginning of the Fascist insurrection and conspiracy, when there was a threatened invasion of the port, the alarm went up. Within an hour the workers were at their posts, ready. In such a huge place that is wonderful. And it reveals wonderful determination!

As a reporter – albeit an openly partisan one – Ethel found again her ability to be detailed and strictly accurate; nowhere more evidently than when she came to write about her own fate in Barcelona. She was never self-pitying, nor even self-important, but saw her own experiences in the light of the revolution and the war at large.

But that drama was some months away yet. For the moment she was a young woman in the most exciting place on earth at the time. Her exhilaration reads like Orwell's first impressions: 'When one came straight from England, the aspect of Barcelona was something startling and overwhelming', or the memories of Antonia Fontanillas, 70 years later, recalling the city of her late teens: 'There was this word *fraternizar* which became very popular. Fraternity, it was all about fraternity. At the beginning that was wonderful.'

And why wouldn't Ethel, Orwell and Antonia be exhilarated? The most radical revolution in recent history – since the European revolutions of 1848 at the very least – was happening all around them. Peasants formed communes on land confiscated from the old ruling elite. Three million men, women and children lived and worked in them. Anarchists had taken over the factories. Police were replaced with civilian self-defence forces. Three quarters of the economy was under anarchist control. Hotels, shops, barber shops and restaurants were collectivised and managed by their workers – often increasing productivity and profit. The maxim 'from each according to his ability, to each according to his need' was put into practice. Women won the right to divorce and abortion, and the idea of 'free love' became popular in the sense that Guy Aldred had been arguing for, the right to enter into a relationship without the permission of State or Church.

∾

*Barcelona, 25th December 1936*

I shall do great things when I am back in Britain, I feel sure, but I want to achieve something here first.

Ethel was full of optimism. Her letters and reports sparkle with the spirit of a joyful young woman on her life's great adventure. She was in her element. She continually remarked on how beautiful Barcelona was. We can imagine her – hardworking and dedicated, getting up early in the mornings to go to the market, observe her fellow citizens, listening to militia men and women, jotting down notes. She found time to take walks with Jenny to the harbour and to eat and drink with new-found comrades in anarchist bars like La Fragua in the Raval, which was typical of the eating houses frequented by anarchist and POUM militia as well as locals: long tables, simple furniture, basic and cheap food – and lots of noise. Bars like these, where Ethel and Jenny would have eaten, acted as unofficial meeting-places for the CNT and the FAI.

Ethel knew she would return one day to Glasgow, but that held no sadness for her either. She loved her adopted Scottish city and had her work to do there. But, for the moment, she lived and breathed and talked – and wrote – Barcelona: 'According to the French papers, Barcelona was to be bombarded last night. But this morning when I awoke, Barcelona was still as beautiful as ever.'

Then, as now, Barcelona had a unique blend of advantages. The second-largest city in Spain, prosperous (in Spanish terms for the time), it teemed with life and movement and colour. Those colours were very different from Glasgow's or Motherwell's: a tender blue sky on sunny days, and a creaminess even in the rain – the elegant buildings' blond stone less blemished by heavy industry. It is a metropolis that sits on a magnificent vantage point. Look one way, and there is the sea; turn around and there are hills, chief amongst them Montjuïc, topped by its confident, French Gothic-style museum.

If Ethel ever commented on Barcelona architects like Antoni Gaudí, her words have not survived. But she must surely have been intrigued by the mix of Art Nouveau and fairytale gothic of the Sagrada Família, dreamed up by an obsessive Catholic. She would have heard the music of the sardana, and watched people dancing to it, holding hands, in a circle, a moving image of unity and solidarity.

The area in which Ethel would have spent the most time is the old town that spirals off Las Ramblas. This was the hub of Barcelona, not only geographically but also politically: all the anarchist organisations, schools and meeting points were based here. It was easy to get lost in the maze of narrow, cheek-by-jowl streets where, in the 1930s, skilled and un-skilled tradesmen, shop assistants, cleaners and people who, until recently, had been unemployed lived, worked and social-ised. This was also where the cheapest cafes and eating-houses were found. The origins of this area known as the Raval are medieval, and today the sun still sends crooked fingers of light down through the higgledy-piggledy rooftops onto cobbled lanes difficult to negotiate after nightfall. At the time, it was the most densely populated urban area in the world.

The Raval was, from the early 1920s onwards, an immig-rant area, attracting workers from the rest of Spain, who tended to be illiterate and very poor. It was here that the anarchists provided education and community support and found volunteers for the militias. Its popular name, Barrio Chino, came from the quarter's similar feel to San Francisco's Chinatown, in vogue in the 1920s through film and novels. Being poor, and an immigrant centre, it too had its gangs and crime, and it was the red-light area of the city. The anarchists set up women's colleges here to counteract the trade. For them, prostitution was another method by which traditional – Catholic – Spain subjugated women and paralysed them politically. No clergyman or practising Catholic, naturally, would condone prostitution, but neither had any effective measure been taken, outside of small, localised charitable work, to tackle the problem and free the women on a major scale. The anarchists provided sex education, girls' and women's literacy centres, and worked with the women's clients in an effort to make them see the reality of the industry they were supporting. The posters of the time are striking: bold, bright handbills, not denouncing women for their evil ways, but looking forward to a bright future, liberated from their dangerous trade and their male buyers. There were poster campaigns too, educating all concerned with the health perils of prostitution through slogans such as 'Venereal diseases are as dangerous as Fascist bullets!' As a result, Barcelona's sex workers were enthusiastic supporters of the revolution.

María Dolors Genovés, professor at Barcelona's Universitat Ramón Llull walked with me along the same streets that Ethel explored in the 1930s, describing the topography of the city Ethel knew. 'The CNT–FAI area was a triangle in the old town, with the Columbus monument, behind us, at its centre,' she explained. 'Here, at the end of the Rambla, is where some of the main offices of the CNT could be found. Later they extended to the Paralelo, the Via Laietana (which was renamed back then the Via Durruti after the anarchist leader), where the headquarters of the Catalan business had been.'

The FAI brought together all anarchist and like-minded groups in Spain and Portugal, functioning as a semi-clandestine organisation of conscious, political anarchists who operated within the CNT. Whereas the CNT was itself a trade union, the FAI was its political arm and organised the anarchist militias. People like Buenaventura Durruti were at the very heart of it.

~

Thirty-year-old Buenaventura Durruti had, before the war, been arrested and jailed several times for his political activities. He had been exiled in France, then Belgium, and finally Spanish Guinea. But the Republic had never managed to control his activities or stem his support among the people. He had been influential in persuading anarchists to not only support the Popular Front in the 1936 elections but also join the Republican government itself. In July of that year he was centrally involved in organising the defeat of the Nationalists in the Barcelona barracks. When Ethel was in Barcelona, Durruti was in Madrid helping form and organize the anti-fascist militias, having already led an army of 3,000 anarchists – the legendary 'Durruti Column' – to the front in Aragon.

'On 19 November 1936, Durruti and his company were in the university campus of Madrid,' Professor Genovés told me. 'A bullet hit him in the chest. He died at dawn on 20 November. There are three theories surrounding his death. One is that anarchists themselves killed him – radical anarchists who were against the CNT–FAI being part of the government. The second is that he was a victim of the counter-revolution – that is to say, the communists assassinated him. The third is that his own gun killed him. Durruti always carried a small pistol, which went off when he got out of a car. The real cause of Durruti's death remains open.'

To this day, communists prefer the theory of an internal anarchist assassination; anarchists, that the communists were the executioners.

On 28 November, Ethel wrote, 'You will have heard of [Durruti's] death. Jenny and I were at the internment. The streets of Barcelona were packed and it was impossible to move . . . It is a terrible business . . . [His] dynamic integrity is a serious loss to the workers' struggle. Except for the knowledge that liberty *does* survive the death of its prophets and its warriors, one would wonder what would come of such a loss . . . His body rested all night in the hall of our Headquarters. We honour his memory, and the uniqueness of his energy and courage combined.'

Regarding Durruti's death, George Orwell wrote in *Homage to Catalonia*, 'To anyone who had been there from the beginning it probably seemed, in December or January, that the revolutionary period was ending.' Ethel was there to catch the last glory days of the anarchist experiment, study it, and record the odd little events that daily life threw up.

'A funny thing happened yesterday,' she noted. 'The door bell rang in the house where we were staying. I answered the bell. Who should it be but the British Consul! I did not recognise him at first, but when he spoke Spanish, his accent was so obvious that I said, "Do you speak English?"

'Then I knew him. He was enquiring for some other folk

and I do not think he remembered *me*. He is very polite and anxious to serve but we did not want him hanging around when we are anxious about the Spanish struggle and the Socialist development of Europe.'

That may sound a little self-important, but Ethel was merely reflecting the truth of the British position before and throughout the Civil War. In the summer of 1936, the consulate in Barcelona had handed to the CNT a list of nearly 100 companies in Catalonia where Britain had 'economic interests'. They were to be protected against collectivisation. The CNT agreed – to the outrage of many of its members, and particularly of the radical FAI. In this, at least, the anarchists showed they were aware of the importance of if not British support then at least its non-intervention in the war. The consul 'dropping in' on Ethel and Jenny presented them with a tricky situation. They were surrounded by people who were in Spain illegally, to fight in a war in which Britain was effectively neutral.

Ethel's dealings with the consulate would soon become very complicated, but for the moment she was satisfied that the visit was purely accidental. 'It was funny as well as strange. Of all the houses in this huge building, he had to come to this one!'

Ethel and Jenny had absolutely no money while they were in Spain. The articles they wrote for the political press brought in nothing, and Ethel's work for the mainstream Scottish newspapers was piecemeal and paid very little. Even the cheap eateries like La Fragua stretched their resources. But lack of funds did not bother Ethel in the least. Comparing themselves to better-off young women in Barcelona, Ethel wrote of herself and Jenny: 'Pretty poor adventuresses, I'm afraid! I thought adventuresses went about in silks and satins, furs and jewels. Jenny and I, if this is the case, must be miserable blacklegs!'

In November, Ethel and Jenny met a legendary figure. 'Emma Goldman introduced herself to us today. But we did not say much.' Goldman had already been informed of their presence, however: 'She knew that there were two comrades from Glasgow and she had heard us speak English.'

Goldman was the most famous – and infamous – anarchist of the period between the wars. Lithuanian by birth, she had originally supported the Russian Revolution, but quickly became disillusioned. 'I could never live my life within the confines of a State,' she had said. She came to world attention when she was arrested in the USA for alleged involvement in the killing of President McKinley in 1901. In fact, she took no part in the assassination, but refused to condemn the anarchist perpetrator Leon Czolgosz. J. Edgar Hoover had called her 'the most dangerous woman in America'.

Goldman's reason for being in Spain was more than simply to support the anarchist movement there. At a speech made at the International Working Men's Association in Paris in 1937, she questioned the decisions of those like Durruti, who encouraged anarchists to join the Republican government:

I have seen from the moment of my first arrival in September 1936 that our comrades in Spain are plunging head foremost into the abyss of compromise that will lead them far away from their revolutionary aim . . . The participation of the CNT–FAI in the government, and concessions to the insatiable monster in Moscow, have certainly not benefited the Spanish Revolution, or even the anti-fascist struggle . . . The revolution in Spain was the result of a military and fascist conspiracy . . . the Spanish workers and peasants soon came to see that their enemies were not only Franco and his Moorish hordes. They soon found themselves besieged by formidable armies and an array of modern arms furnished to Franco by Hitler and Mussolini . . . Thus finding themselves up against a stone wall, the CNT–FAI was forced to descend from its lofty traditional heights to compromise right and left: participation in the government, all sorts of humiliating overtures to Stalin, superhuman tolerance for his henchmen who were openly plotting and conniving against the Spanish Revolution . . . No, I have not changed my attitude toward government as an evil. As all through my life, I still hold that the State is a cold monster, and that it devours everyone within its reach . . . With Franco at the gate of Madrid, I could hardly blame the CNT–FAI for choosing a lesser evil – participation in the government rather than dictatorship, the most deadly evil.

Goldman took the two Scotswomen to see areas of the city they hadn't visited before. 'The other day the great Emma Goldman took Jenny and me to see a hospital, purely under CNT control. All the staff are comrades and share alike. The place was formerly a nunnery and it was decided to transform it into a hospital!' From the beginning of January, Ethel travelled beyond the confines of the Barrio Gótico and the Raval, writing about what she saw.

*4th January 1937*

I am told that life in the villages where they have Libertarian Communism is wonderful. I am going to try and get away to one of them to see what the life is really like.

Within a few days she had made the journey.

Yesterday, Sunday, I went to a small place outside Barcelona called Sabadell. Here, I met a few Spanish comrades and was in a few Spanish houses. Some of those are beyond description. But the spirit of the Spanish comrades is good. In this place a group of young comrades have taken over a house and there they have a school for mutual instruction. I am going there again to spend a whole day with them.

What Ethel experienced in Sabadell impressed her enormously. She was a city girl herself, her political formation the result of living in Scotland's industrial heartland. Anarchism in rural areas had its own traditions, and, though different factions of the movement throughout the province and indeed in all the anarchist areas of Spain generally united and worked together in 1936, the history and experience of the countryside was very different from that of Barcelona.

*Barcelona, 11th January 1937*

I want to tell you about yesterday, Sunday. I went again to Sabadell, a little town about 20 kilometres from Barcelona and which is a very important place viewed from the standpoint of the trains conveying people to Barcelona. The comrade with whom I went was on guard there during the 19th of July – the day the Military rose across Spain but was defeated in the Catalan capital.

We went to the house of one comrade who is Minister of War in Sabadell. Then with another comrade, Jara, who works for him in that department. We journeyed by car to another town called Castellar, about 10 kilometres from Sabadell. There we had, in the usual Spanish fashion, Vermouth and potato crisps. Back in Sabadell we had lunch with Jara. We talked about the movement, and I have discovered that the Spanish Anarchists are truly a liberty loving people and have definite ideas of action – not mere theory!

After eating we went to a café where all the comrades gather and again I was impressed with the sympathy we have for them in their ideas. They really are Anarchists! Another comrade took us to the headquarters of the FAI in Sabadell. This was a convent and is now used for various propaganda purposes. They have converted one room into a lecture room which will hold about 1,000 people. Very up-to-date for an old convent!

Many comrades of the FAI stay there and the work goes on – repairing things, etc. The convents and monasteries of Spain have come in very handy.

There is a breathlessness about Ethel's writing during these first few months. As she races from meeting to meeting and town to town, her fascination for the people she meets and the work being done overrides any real attempt at analysis.

Andrew and Daisy Macdonald at Calder Road, Bellshill, 1940s.

| No. | Name and Surname. | When and Where Born. | Sex. | Name, Surname, and Rank or Profession of Father. Name, and Maiden Surname of Mother. Date and Place of Marriage. | Signature and Qualification of Informant, and Residence, if out of the House in which the Birth occurred. | When and Where Registered, and Signature of Registrar. |
|---|---|---|---|---|---|---|
| 272 | Camelia Ethel McDonald | 190 9 February Twenty fourth 9·20 a.m. 20·7 Windmill Hill Street Sutherwood | 7 | Andrew McDonald Coach Driver (Journeyman) Daisy McDonald M.S. Hatton 1907 August 26. Brentford | (Signed) Andrew McDonald Father Present | 190 9. February 21. At Dalziel (Signed) Registrar |

Extracted from the Register Book of Births, for the Parish of Dalziel ............ in the
County of ............ this 24 day of February .......... 190 9 ⅄ John D. Robb Asst. Registrar

Camelia Ethel's birth certificate.

Ethel, in her late teens.

Young Guy Aldred.

Smoke rises over Barcelona after air raids by General Franco's Nationalist forces, March 1936.
*Getty Images*

A militiawoman holding high ground on the Aragon Front against the rebels. *Getty Images*

Dolores Ibarruri, 'La Pasionaria'. *Getty Images*

¿WHAT ARE YOU DOING

TO PREVENT THIS?

MADRID

MINISTERIO DE PROPAGANDA

Ministry of Propaganda poster (1936/7) to galvanize international support for the Republic.
*University of California, San Diego.*

C.N.T. COMITE NACIONAL A.I.T.

OFICINA DE
INFORMACION
Y PROPAGANDA

FASCISMO

CNT poster, produced in conjunction with the UGT, during the early months of the war.
*University of California, San Diego.*

Ministry of Propaganda, 1936. The artist, Juan Antonio Morales, depicts the elements of Nationalist support: a bishop, an Italian Fascist soldier, Moroccan conscripts and a capitalist wearing Nazi insignia. *University of California, San Diego.*

Juan Miró's 1937 poster was used to rouse support in France. *University of California, San Diego.*

Mujeres Libres poster: 'Your family is everyone who fights for Liberty!'

Anti-prostitution poster: 'There is a new life for you, offering dignified work and a human existence'

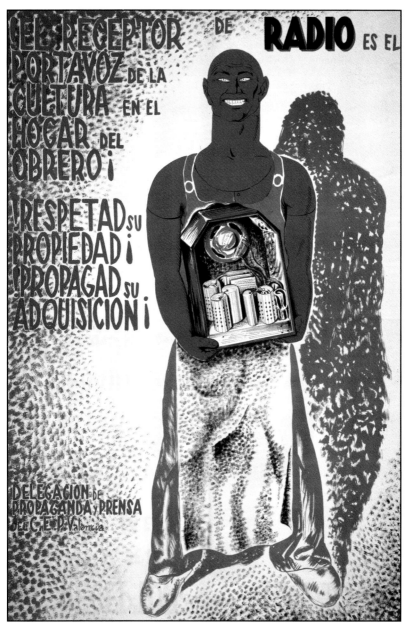

'The radio receiver is the mouthpiece of culture in the home of the worker! Respect it! Everyone should have one'. UGT CNT poster, 1936. *University of California, San Diego.*

## Comrades Listen In ! ! !

———

BARCELONA RADIO (CNT),
Station ECNI. Short wave 42.88;
Normal 222.55, English Talk, every
night, by ETHEL MACDONALD
(Glasgow United Socialist Move-
ment), at 10.30.

RADIO P.O.U.M.
Station E.C.P.2.—42 meters.

English every night at 8.
Greenwich time.

Announcement giving times of Ethel's talks from Spain.

Graphic Republican poster

Ethel on her lecture tour after her
return from Spain

Guernica, after the Condor Legion bombing, April 1937.
*Getty Images*

*Above.* Ethel visiting home, perhaps for the last time. Clockwise from centre front: Ethel, Guy, Caldy, unknown, unknown, Jenny.

*Right.* Bessie (Elizabeth), Freddie's mother and Ethel's younger sister, in her ATS uniform at the start of the Second World War.

*Below.* 'Wee' Freddie, with his dad, Freddie, and mother, Ethel's sister, Bessie.

She is aware of the fact herself:

> Perhaps I do not give you a very clear idea of what is happening. But, as a comrade said to me, one gets impressions and it is very difficult to either speak or write about them.
>
> After leaving the FAI headquarters we went to the house of the comrades whom we visited last week. There are María – a woman about 45, typically Spanish – three other women, María, Janet and Josephine. Also, Juan, Domingo and Pepito. And a dog and two cats and a baby. We ate, and drank the beautiful Spanish wine. And we talked. I shall go again and again and each time I shall understand better.

The Janet can't be right. Perhaps a Lana or Joana, or a woman known by her mother's name, beginning with 'Ll', which in Catalan is pronounced like our J. Ethel's Spanish was still limited, but her desire to 'understand better' was sincere. 'I long for Sundays,' she writes at the end of her missive, 'to get back to Sabadell,' and, for as long as she was able, she returned regularly.

Just how profound the social and economic changes were in rural areas is still a matter of debate and research. So little attention has been paid to the revolution of 1936, lost in the general narrative of the Civil War, that key facts and events still await clarification. Not long after her arrival, Ethel had written home: 'Jenny and I are truly alright. What we need is money. That medium is in use here still . . .' Her point was that it was believed, both in Barcelona itself and well beyond, that a barter system had replaced coinage. 'Outside Barcelona in the smaller towns and villages money is not used.'

María Dolors Genovés thinks this is something of a myth, but one based on certain realities. From the moment the revolution started to expand throughout central Catalonia and the coast, some anarchist groups stopped using the normal currency. Instead, they reverted to the ancient system of exchanging goods and services. There is no doubt that some collectives adopted a barter system, trading wine for wheat, for example. Whether or not, had the revolution been given time to develop, that barter would have taken hold, we can't say. But the very fact that, in some areas at least, the barter system enjoyed a brief revival is indicative of the ambition of the Catalan anarchists.

There is no doubt the extraordinary social changes that continue to inspire today were brought about by poor farmers and agricultural workers. For Noam Chomsky, reading about Catalonia roused him politically as a young man. '[It was] maybe the most successful case of people actually taking their lives into their own hands. I remember as a child, in about 1940, when I was just learning about these things, reading the documents of the collectives. Some of them are very moving. There's one in particular – a village called Membrilla which, in the documents written at the time, describes itself as the poorest village in Spain – but the most *just*.'

Back in Barcelona, Ethel was in touch with many of the *brigadistas*, those volunteers who had either just arrived from their home countries, or were on leave from the Aragon front. Among them was Charles Doran, a Glaswegian and a World War I veteran, who had not long left Scotland and was about to go off and fight alongside Orwell in the POUM.

*Barcelona, 14th January 1937*

Charlie Doran is sitting here at present, telling me all about Glasgow and Lanarkshire. He came the day before yesterday with the ILP section from London, and here he is attached to the POUM.

I think it is bad that someone does not take over arrangements for sending comrades with Anarchist tendencies, or who at least are anti-CP, from Britain to Spain.

Charlie Doran was one of several ILP members who went to Spain under their own steam, ahead of the planned ILP Contingent. Increasing pressure from the London Government meant that the eventual Contingent numbered only 25, rather than the intended 130 fighting men. The ILP members, including George Orwell, fought alongside the POUM, earning them accusations of 'counter-revolution' by communists. The CPGB and the ILP had been trading insults and accusations since the outset of the war.

The initiative for the International Brigades was largely mobilised by the Communist Party, which, as we have seen, had been actively recruiting worldwide since autumn 1936, via a series of meetings encouraging young working-class men – and a significant number of women, many of whom served in medical units – to go to Spain and fight for the Republic out of international solidarity. As a result, most volunteers, when they arrived, were attached to communist militias and brigades. Catalan anarchists, controlling the border with France, had initially attempted to stop communist-affiliated volunteers from entering the country, until protests, including from amongst their own movement, put a stop to the practice. Many of the men, however, were neither members nor supporters of the Communist Party, but ended up fighting alongside them. Equally, some *brigadistas* fought in CNT and POUM militias without being either anarchist or Trotskyist.

'Doran paid his own fare,' Ethel pointed out. The anarchist movement in Europe simply did not have the money to send volunteers to Spain.

> And why does someone not impress on the British volunteers not to get drunk when they arrive here? There is always that tendency. Perhaps it is because they are unaccustomed to wine.
>
> Despite the fact that one can obtain all kinds of wines and spirits here very cheaply, I have never yet seen a Spaniard drunk, or even tipsy. Certainly the Continent is an argument against prohibition. Doran was very indignant at the idea of volunteers for freedom getting drunk. I sympathise with his feelings.

No doubt cheap wine was a problem. But there were other factors too. These men, many of them very young, were about to go into battle for the first time. Dutch courage was needed as much as rebel spirit. In the main, volunteers were from working-class backgrounds and had probably never travelled far from home. Being in Spain was every bit as much an adventure for them as it was for Ethel. Their excitement in meeting like-minded friends from all over the world on the eve of joining the front to battle with fascists must have been considerable – it is hardly surprising, therefore, that they enjoyed themselves while they could in revolutionary Barcelona.

The International Brigades remain, nearly 70 years later, the most potent symbol of the Spanish Civil War. In a less clearly defined world, the notion of people travelling from all over the globe, often under very difficult conditions, to get to Spain and fight, still moves us. Between 35,000 to 40,000 people joined the brigades, including 2,400 Britons. Of them, 549 were Scots – twice as many per head of population as the rest of the UK. Nearly 10,000 volunteers of all nationalities never returned. Some came from Germany and Italy – we can only imagine what they had to go through to smuggle themselves out of their fascist-controlled countries. When the war ended and they returned, they went back for the most part to their deaths.

With the exception of the first day they arrived in Spain, and short periods of leave from fighting, the international volunteers did not have much time to enjoy themselves. According to Professor Willy Maley, volunteers like his father, who remembers leaving for Spain from George Square in double-decker buses, were 'treated relatively well until they got captured – or killed'. Once they arrived in Spain most were given six weeks' training. The fighting, on every front, was vicious and often chaotic. 'You have to remember that the Spanish Civil War was, on the one hand, very modern. It involved the total flattening of towns – think, for instance of the bombing of Guernica. That was a precursor of Fallujah. On the other hand you had the last cavalry charge in modern military history. Moroccan soldiers on horseback who encircled and captured the machine-gun company after they'd run out of ammunition.'

The war being waged in Spain was very different to that which the soldiers had experienced. On the Republican side, largely, it was not organised and conducted by army professionals – they were fighting the Spanish army, which had rebelled against the democratically elected Republic. Republican forces were made up of the butcher, the baker, the peasant and the urban worker. This was a new kind of army emerging from a new society. Workers' militias were born in factories and fields, and members were armed with whatever kind of weapons they had to hand. In Madrid, people had to forge makeshift arms out of melted-down railings.

The extent of women's involvement in the actual business of fighting is still a matter of debate. It was probably less than has sometimes been suggested, but there certainly were, particularly among the anarchists, combative women's militias.

Women's lives, in general, had changed profoundly in recent years. Until the early 1930s, the position of women in Spanish society had been as bad, or worse, than in Scotland. They had been paid half the meagre wages of men – less than two pesetas a day, often for precisely the same work. Arranged marriages were common, and unmarried women had to be accompanied by chaperones. The Republic had passed a series of laws which had begun to change the situation. Divorce, for example, albeit in exceptional circumstances, was allowed. In Catalonia the changes were more fundamental: automatic equal share of property whether or not there was an official State or Church marriage; the introduction of civil marriage itself; wider rights to divorce and to abortion.

In 1936, anarchist women founded their own pressure group, Mujeres Libres (Free Women). Mujeres Libres called for equal pay – and in many collectives they were successful. For the first time in Spanish history, women had a real say, politically, economically and in the home. Mujeres Libres numbered 30,000 female members at its height. They set up women's colleges in Barcelona, which, by 1938, were taking in 600 to 800 female students per day. They opened maternity hospitals and schools, and co-ordinated military training. The Spanish term *mi mujer*, meaning 'my wife', but literally 'my woman', was replaced by *mi compañera*. From a feminist perspective, Mujeres Libres was the most innovative and clear-headed women's organisation in existence during the Civil War, although not all of its members, or even its leaders, counted themselves as 'feminists'. It fostered radical views on sexual and family relations, campaigned against the exploitation of women in prostitution, encouraged female workers to join trade unions and engage in political activity, and generally promoted the image of a new, independent, trained, working woman.

Antonia Fontanillas, in her little flat in Dreux, avidly remembers both the colleges themselves and the changes in women's lives they brought about: 'In the old convent of Viladomat Street and Gran Via, they created the first popular university which then became the Instituto Libre (Free Institute).

'I remember there was a young girl, very well dressed; I found it really strange that this girl could not read. She had never been to school! At first I'd thought [Mujeres Libres] was just for women older than me, in their thirties or older.

Being so young at the time, I never really thought about all that. Then I met some of these "free women". I started buying their newspaper and the magazine, and realised how important it was what they were doing.'

Antonia told me a little story that demonstrates the difference education and political involvement made to girls like her. 'The young women where I worked had this silly idea of buying hats and wearing them to work. At that time only the bourgeoisie, the well-off middle-class ladies, wore hats. Really, it was a big change.

'What Mujeres Libres really wanted was to encourage the ordinary girl. Show her she had a role in society. We were women, but first we were individuals. You have the right to choose your own life. You're no longer condemned to be at home. You don't have to become a mother. You have the right to be whatever you want to be.'

Inspired by all of these changes, Ethel Macdonald became increasingly exasperated not only with British foreign policy, but even her beloved workers' inability to see the importance of the battle being waged. 'I have faith in the British worker. But he is a bit slow isn't he?' She herself could not be busier: 'I am typing this in the bureau and a meeting is about to commence.'

Time was running out, although it would be two more years before Franco's troops mounted his offensive against Barcelona. The city would not fall until 1939. But, even at the start of 1937, with sporadic fighting in Aragon, and Falangist troops coming ever closer to Madrid, the situation seemed critical. And there was another need for urgency, much nearer to home. The uneasy alliance between the communists – every day more powerful within the Republic both in Madrid and Barcelona – and the anarchists, was becoming increasingly strained. Each side was running out of patience with the other. Orwell had remarked that the 'revolutionary period' was already over. The atmosphere was getting worse with each passing day. 'Under the seeming gaiety of the streets,' he wrote, 'with their flower stalls, their propaganda posters, and thronging crowds, there was an unmistakable and horrible feeling of political rivalry and hatred . . .'

Ethel knew as well as Orwell that a confrontation was brewing between those who, in her opinion, wished to defend, and enlarge, the revolution, and those who wanted to stop it in its tracks. Her hostility towards the Communist Party features regularly in her own writing of the time: 'Today there was a demonstration to celebrate the Russian Revolution. Same old CP everywhere! The CNT mainly joined in the demonstration, but Jenny and I, with the French and German sections, did not participate. [We] went to the harbour and enjoyed sun-ray treatment instead!'

In a speech in January 1937, Santiago Carrillo, the General Secretary of the Spanish Communist Party made their position clear: 'There are some who say that at this stage we should fight for the socialist revolution, and there are others who say that we are practising a deception, manoeuvring to conceal our real policy when we declare that we are defending the democratic republic. Comrades, we *are* fighting for a democratic republic and, furthermore, for a *parliamentary* republic.'

This, to Ethel and Jenny Patrick, was anathema. The CNT–FAI responded with: 'It should be clearly understood that we are *not* fighting for the democratic republic. We are fighting for the triumph of the proletarian revolution. The revolution and the war are inseparable. Everything that is said to the contrary is counter-revolution.'

Soon, Ethel's voice – quite literally – would be heard louder and more often. 'Will Jenny and I achieve our ambitions?' she asked in one of her early letters home. 'She tells me of the movement's expectations as to me speaking . . . I hope I shall become a speaker. An able and intelligent speaker, and not just one who speaks. I shall do my best. I *want* to speak and this is an experience that should enable me to do so.'

In those early months in Barcelona she wrote her articles for home consumption, and endlessly urged action: 'Without your British Government's consent,' she scolded her readers, '[Franco's army] could never have been brought across the Mediterranean. Without your apathy the Moorish troops would never have entered Spain. English-speaking workers, why are you sleeping while your Spanish brothers and sisters and comrades are being murdered?! Where are your traditions? Speak! *Act*!'

# 6

# *The Voice of Anarchism*

*∼ Workers – act! The Spanish workers are holding the pass. They cannot hold it forever. Will you not rally to their assistance? Will you not defeat Fascism?! ∼*

With the Spanish Civil War came an abundance of poster art. 'The walls of the city,' said one observer, 'became an anti-fascist art gallery.' Virtually every building, every billboard, gable end and harbour wall supported big, bright images. Red and black flags blew atop every second lamppost and telegraph pole; highly coloured leaflets and newssheets were quickly produced and widely distributed. The posters in particular were genuine works of art. Borrowing style and sinew from the illustrations and paintings of the Russian Revolution, they combined very Catalan Art Nouveau techniques with the graphics of German expressionism. They played with the aggressive romanticism of Nazi propaganda, turning mythological racism on its head. Spanish propaganda design in the 1930s pre-shadowed the Pop Art of the 1960s and the poster art of revolutions to come.

More than 2,000 individual posters were designed in the run up to and during the war. A palace that had belonged to an aristocratic family was requisitioned and turned into a studio and meeting place for artists. There they met and found ways to address every social and military problem facing the ordinary citizen. They created posters for the Ministry of Agriculture, showing for instance a *campesino* spearing a fascist cobra, holding his sickle in his left hand: 'Use Your Weapons to Defend the Government that Gave You Your Land!' The Socialist Party demanded, in Catalan, 'Strong Men – Go to the Front!' Some designs were extraordinarily explicit, such as the illustration of two Swastika-emblazoned bombs about to strike the heart of an already dead, bleeding (and scantily clad) woman.

There was humour too – in one image, the Nationalists are depicted, with their suits and mitres and medals, on a leaky boat, bearing only one decrepit canon, and being steered by a fez-bedecked Moroccan soldier. And there was hope: 'The Revolution has Colours' is a beautiful and uplifting piece of art which, despite the hardship and danger of the times, goes on to assert: 'Not all is combat, death, war, blood, pain. There is also happiness, life, youth. Our Spanish revolution is built on joy and youthfulness. That is why it will triumph.'

Posters commissioned by Mujeres Libres address the position and role of the female population. Many of them have the capacity to move the viewer even now, three quarters of a century on. On one poster, two emaciated street-walkers are called on to recognise that there is a new world now, one in which they can have 'Work with Dignity, and a Decent Life.' Another announces 'The CNT – Liberator of Prostitutes'.

Designs by people like Josep Renau were truly experimental, influencing Picasso, Miró and a whole generation to come. Picasso himself was appointed director of the Prado Museum just after the outbreak of war, and in 1937 began work on his masterpiece *Guernica*. Joan Miró, as well as producing his famous 'Red and Black' series of etchings, a surrealist nightmare of rising fascism, also designed some of the most optimistic posters of the Civil War, including *Aidez Espagne*, appealing for French support. Other posters were aimed at foreign countries and sympathisers, including the plea in English, 'What Are You Doing to Prevent This?' showing a mother and baby cowering under German planes in the siege of Madrid.

However, the tensions between the anarchists and the communists could be read even in their art. The Communist Party released banners and handbills insisting: 'First the War, Then the Revolution', clearly a criticism of the CNT. The Anarchist Union, for its part, put up posters depicting the gains of the revolution. One in particular, an industrial angel, dog-fighting in the sky with fascist planes, is an inspiration for Antony Gormley's *Angel of the North* sculpture in Gateshead. Both movements used La Pasionaria's famous declaration, '*No pasarán!*'

Writers, too, put their energies into defending the Republic and, sometimes, the revolution. Rafael Alberti's communist poems are a departure from his surrealist style. Federico García Lorca's poems like 'Ballad of the Spanish Civil Guard' were powerful denunciations of militarist society. Lorca was, of course, killed by Nationalist militia in the summer of 1936. Poets from outside Spain wrote passionately of the struggle, the Chilean Pablo Neruda and Peruvian César Vallejo amongst them. *Brigadistas* too wrote of their experiences, including the Irish communist Thomas O'Brian and the English poets John Cornford and W.H. Auden. The latter served first in Spain as an ambulance driver, but, like Ethel, took up a position broadcasting from the thick of the war.

Radio was the newest, fastest, and most powerful medium of the time, its potential quickly harnessed by the military on both sides. A poster, issued by the Delegation for Propaganda in Valencia was resolute (and persistent) about the reach of broadcasting: on it, a worker holds a radio set, its innards resembling an explosion, over a cityscape. The text reads, 'Radio is the loudspeaker of Culture in your home, Worker! Respect it! Make sure every home has one!'

The radio set in the kitchen was becoming as important a weapon in Spain's ideological struggle as the gun. Radio broadcasts brought people together, animated them for battles ahead and soothed troubled spirits. Its military applications were legion: holding units together, gathering data and spreading information and misinformation. Radio was the most compelling and potent communication tool of the day. And, just as it changed the nature of the war, war impacted on the future of broadcasting – for good and ill. A British journalist in 1937 reported back that the Spanish war was bringing about a complete metamorphosis of radio.

The Nationalists made extremely effective use of the technology even from before their uprising in July 1936. They drummed up fear of the rebel army's approach before attacking a town, threatening terrible reprisals for those who put up resistance. They exaggerated their previous victories, and the weapons at their disposal. They created, through broadcasts, mental pictures of the Great Liberator – Franco – entering cities and towns on a white horse, punishing Republicans.

The Republican forces for their part used the medium more within their own areas, broadcasting warnings of attacks and the successful defence of cities and regions. For the first time in history, soldiers and civilians on all sides of the battle, at home and at the front, could communicate, and be communicated with. Within months of the outbreak of war, every station in Spain was directly controlled either by the rebels or the loyalists and used solely for the dissemination of propaganda and military communication.

In Catalonia, the CNT station was crucial for volunteers. Communicating between the various militias, with all the languages spoken by international volunteers, had been problematic. Radio was the one tool at their disposal which could spread news and calls to arms quickly, and in different languages. Spanish was the lingua franca – militia from all over Spain could understand and so too could the vast majority of Catalans. But English was just as important, the one language that French, Germans, Italians and Belgians might understand.

English was also necessary in order to broadcast beyond the confines of Spain, to put the Republican and anarchist positions to the world and to notify the international community both of their successes and of the peril they were facing in the advancing Nationalist army. Short-wave radio technology developed rapidly in the 1930s, allowing signals to be broadcast vast distances. Programmes from Barcelona could now be picked up across the world.

Ethel's journalistic and propaganda skills had been noticed at CNT headquarters. When the Anarchist Union launched an English-language service, they looked specifically for a woman to front it. And so, in 1937, Ethel Macdonald, Knowetop Primary School lassie, Motherwell shop girl, now aged 28 and barely three months in Spain, became the international voice of anarchist Barcelona.

'The English language is held by those who speak it to be the great language of freedom,' she said in one of her first transmissions.

> Democrats forget that Charles I and other upholders of tyranny and the divine right of kings, centralised State oppression, spoke in the English tongue. They think only of John Hampden, of Milton, of Richard Carlisle, of George Washington, not as slave-dealer but challenger of the British monarchy; of Thomas Paine, of Abraham Lincoln at Gettysburg . . . Martyrs for freedom and pioneers of liberty, equality and democracy.
>
> To all who believe, therefore, in the best of the English tongue; who hear in it the ringing accents of the martyrs and not the callous cynical tones of the persecutor and judge, I address myself.

There are pictures of Ethel, sometimes sitting and sometimes standing, behind the radio station's large electro-voice microphones. We can imagine her, chain-smoking, her notepads and papers beside her, ink on her fingers, explaining to her near neighbours, as well as unknown people on the other side of the world, the drama that she found herself playing so active a part in.

'I ask you again to make it the language of freedom. Let it vie with the Spanish tongue, and the tongue of one-time revolutionary France. Let it speak to Fascism! To Hitler, to Mussolini, and to Franco. Let the voice of the people of England, the voice of strangled freedom be heard!'

No recordings of Ethel's broadcasts, as far as I can discover, were made, or at any rate preserved, but there are some scripts, and numerous references – in Spain, the UK and the United States – to her clear and warm tone, the composure of her broadcasting style and the clarity of her arguments.

> Tomorrow, Saturday the 20th of February, 1937, is the date fixed by the sub-committee of non-intervention, sitting in London, for the commencement of the ban on volunteers for Spain. Volunteers to Spain! From where have these volunteers come? Italy has sent, not volunteers, but conscripts. Germany landed in Spanish territory, not volunteers, but conscripts. The army of rebel Franco consists, not of volunteers, but of conscript Moors, conscript Germans, conscript Italians, all bent on making Spain a Fascist colony and Africa a Fascist hell, with the defeat and the retreat of democracy everywhere . . .

A week before this broadcast, Malaga fell to the rebel generals. Four days later, international volunteers helped halt their advance on Madrid in the terrible battles at Jarama. The subject of military volunteers and the democratic powers' policy on the war was crucial. Ethel was clear that bourgeois parliaments could never be relied upon to help: 'Parliamentarianism is the road to militarism . . . Belief in parliament does not lead to freedom, but to the emancipation of a few selected persons at the expense of the whole of the working class.

'What are the actions of the parliamentary parties with regard to support of the Spanish struggle? They talk, they discuss, they speak with bated breath of the horrors that are taking place in Spain. They gesticulate, they proclaim to the world their determination to assist Spain and to see that Fascism is halted . . . And that is all they do. Talk.'

In a letter home to Guy her impatience extended even to him. 'Do you remember the proposal about sending a battalion of 50 anarchists from Glasgow? I think you had better start getting your list ready. But they must be *anarchists* or *anti-parliamentarians*! This is essential.'

Over the airways, Ethel had no doubt who her audience was: the soldiers, militiamen and citizens outside the CNT building she was broadcasting from, and like-minded radicals wherever they found themselves. 'Comrades, fellow-workers,' she addressed her unseen listeners; many other people might well have been tuning in, but they did not concern her. Her constituency was the working man and woman who had a great deal to gain, or lose, from the battle waging in Spain.

Comrades, fellow-workers, of what use are your meetings that pass pious resolutions, that exhibit Soldiers of the International Column, provide entertainment, make collections and achieve nothing? This is not the time for sympathy and charity. This is the time for action. Do you not understand that every week, every day and every hour counts? Each hour that passes means the death of more Spanish men and women, and yet you advertise meetings, talk, arrange to talk and fail to take any action. Your leaders ask questions in Parliament, in the Senate, collect in small committees and make arrangements to send clothes and food to the poor people of Spain who are menaced by this horrible monster of Fascism, and in the end, do nothing.

Are you, English-speaking workers, prepared to let this tragic force which means the rape of Spain go on? Are you prepared to lend yourselves to this mockery? If you are men and women, if you sense class struggle, you will permit no ban on volunteers.

Ethel was very aware that the problem of waging war against a much better equipped and organised army was more than simply a question of manpower: 'We welcome every man that comes to Spain to offer his life in the cause of freedom. But of what use are these volunteers if we have no arms to give them? We want arms, ammunition, aeroplanes, all kinds of war material.'

For much of the rest of this broadcast, Ethel not only criticised the Western democracies but gave vent to her anger and impatience with the left itself. Laying the burden of action on ordinary people was, in a sense, Ethel Macdonald's signature tune. From her earliest articles in *Regeneración*, and throughout the rest of her life, she was frustrated by people's inability to act, and to act swiftly. Worse, that they should put any faith into parliaments acting on their behalf. She was, indeed, often as angry with her own comrades as with their governments:

You have permitted Franco to have soldiers and arms and aeroplanes and ammunition. Your governments, in the name of democracy, have starved the government and workers of Spain . . . Your governments, workers of the world, are assisting in the development of fascism. They are conniving at the defeat of the workers' cause, and you tamely accept this, or merely idly protest against it. Workers, your socialism and your communism are worthless. Your democracy is a sham, and that sham is fertilising the fields of Spain with the blood of the Spanish people. Your sham democracy is making the men, women and children of Spain the sod of fascism. The workers of Spain bid you cry, Halt! The workers of Spain bid you act!'

Radio was still in its infancy, but Ethel instinctively discovered its magic very early. This speech is typical of her broadcasts – well constructed, building in logic and intensity. All the reports of those who heard her broadcast talk of the sweetness of her tone and her professional control. They comment on the 'magnetic' quality of her voice; she is never described as ranting or blustering. Her words, however, seldom fail to hit their target:

And you, parliamentarians, you so-called socialists, talk and talk, and know not how to act. Nor when to act. For Spain, you are not even prepared to threaten war. 'Non-intervention', as a slogan, is an improvement on 'Sanctions' – it is even more radically hypocritical! It is more thorough and deliberate lying. For nonintervention means the connived advance of fascism.

This cannot be disputed. Under the cloak of non-intervention, Hitler and Mussolini are being assisted in their wanton destruction of Spain . . . Your governments are not for non-intervention. They stand quite definitely for intervention, intervention on behalf of their friends and allies, Hitler and Mussolini. Your governments and your leaders have many points in common with these two scoundrels. All of them lack decency, human understanding, and intelligence.

It is quite a claim (and one, incidentally, that Noam Chomsky echoes) that Hitler and Mussolini are somehow 'allies' of Britain, France and the United States – the very powers who went to war with them two years later. Yet it must have seemed like this in Barcelona in 1937. The Western democracies, it was felt, were even more terrified of a revolutionary Spain than of a fascist Spain.

Comrades, workers, Malaga has fallen. Malaga was betrayed and you too were betrayed, for you have witnessed not merely the fall of Malaga but the fall of a key defence of world democracy, of workers' struggle, of world liberty, of world emancipation. Malaga fell; you, the world proletariat, were invaded: and you talk. Talk and lament and sigh and fear to act! Tomorrow, Madrid may be bombed once more. Barcelona may be attacked. Valencia may be attacked, and still you talk! When will this talking cease? Will you never act?

The crisis is here. The hour of struggle is here. Now is the decisive moment. By all your traditions of liberty and struggle, by all the brave martyrs of old, in the name of the heroic Spanish men and women,

I bid you act. Act on behalf of Spain through living,
immediate Committees of Action in Britain, in America,
throughout the whole world. Let your cry be not non-
intervention, but 'Hands off Spain'.

Workers of the world! Rally! Think – and act now!

'Comrades Listen In!' reads an advert that was placed in
many British radical magazines and newssheets, including
*Regeneración*. 'Barcelona Radio (CNT), station ECNI. Short
wave 42.88; Normal 222.55. English Talk, every night, by
Ethel Macdonald (Glasgow United Socialist Movement), at
10.30. RADIO POUM Station ECP2 – 42 meters. English
every night at 8. Greenwich time.'

During the period she was broadcasting from Spain,
Ethel's journalistic skills were at their sharpest. For instance,
she dealt with the fall of Malaga, not by attempting to
describe the ferocity of the battle or the brutal repercussions
of Franco's victory, but by telling the story of one non-
combatant man's fate: 'Sir Peter Mitchell has lately returned
to England after having been in residence near Malaga. He
was detained by the forces of Franco when they took the
city. He was only released on the intervention of the British
Government.'

Sir Peter Chalmers Mitchell, a Scot born in Dumfermline,
was elderly and one of the world's greatest zoologists. He
had retired to Malaga in 1932. His experiences in Spain were
brought to public attention by Ethel Macdonald, and by his
close friend, Arthur Koestler who, like Ethel, had gone to
Spain to report on the central ideological showdown of the
twentieth century. Koestler was in Malaga in 1937 following
the plight of the refugees fleeing the Nationalists.

126

'Malaga is bombed from the air at least once a day,' Koestler had written before the final attack. Both he and Mitchell were Republicans and supporters of the Communist Party. Mitchell had used his fame and position to help refugees – from both sides of the conflict – escape the war via British-held Gibraltar. One of them was Koestler himself. The day after the Nationalists' victory the left-wing journalist was arrested. There is no doubt that his life was in grave danger; happily, Mitchell stepped in once again and managed to negotiate the writer's release.

Mitchell's own life and liberty were in danger too – his status could not protect him from Franco for long, especially as he continued to help people escape the country. Ethel, in her article on him, quotes Mitchell as saying: 'I am on forced parole. I am released on the understanding that I would say nothing of what has been happening in Spain.'

Why the secrecy? If Franco had been received – as stated by the Capitalist press – with tears of joy on the part of the population, why should not every person be free to give honour to Fascism?

Malaga is a place of suffering and torment. Fascism does not wish that truth to be told. On the other hand there have been hundreds and thousands of representatives who have come to Spain to see what has actually been taking place. In no instance has the Spanish [Republican] Government demanded secrecy as the payment for their departure. The legitimate forces in Spain have nothing to hide. All is done for the world to see. And for the world to follow.

127

Ethel's broadcasts made their mark in the United States. Some months after her first programmes, when there was concern for her safety, articles appeared in the British press reporting on Ethel's popularity across the Atlantic. Her Scottish accent seemed to be an attraction for American ears.

Certainly, she had an ability to show how events in a distant country had global implications. She spoke, in one broadcast, of 'the brutality and ferocity with which this war is being operated on the part of the Fascists'. The importance of the Civil War to the foreign listener should be clear, 'not merely because of the heroism that the proletariat of Spain is showing in the face of the onslaught by Germany and Italy, but because from this war there is the possibility of a world conflagration ensuing that will have no equal in history'.

One article in the British press relates that a prominent news editor in California had received hundreds of letters about Ethel Macdonald, from all parts of the USA and Canada. Not, one imagines, because they agreed necessarily with what she said on Barcelona Radio, but because she had the 'best radio voice they had ever heard'. (Having said that, an opinion poll carried out in the USA in 1939 found that 87 per cent of Americans hoped for a Republican victory over the Nationalists. Anarchism as an ideology, it shouldn't be forgotten, has a long and significant history in that country.) The article continued, 'Hollywood will be interested to know that Ethel is no ordinary girl – her radio voice is equalled by her magnetic personality ... [she] would take risks cheerfully if she could be of help to others.'

Well, the Hollywood blockbuster is yet to made. The idea is ludicrous – America's anarchist tradition is not *that* widespread. But Ethel's readiness to take risks on behalf of others – so long as they were part of the movement – was about to be proven. The Radio Barcelona broadcasts were extremely successful, but they were also dangerous. Ethel Macdonald was no longer just one of many volunteers, writers and activists in the Catalan capital, but a recognised figure. In the worsening atmosphere of Barcelona an anarchist speaker with the potential to move and inspire was putting herself in a perilous position.

If the media was crucial in the battle between left and right, it was just as crucial in the fight for ideological supremacy between rival anti-fascists. Orwell noted that, in the spring of 1937, it was becoming obvious that working-class control of Barcelona was a lost cause. The alliance between communists in their increasingly powerful Unified Socialist Party of Catalonia (PSUC) and the anarchists was just as obviously falling apart. The talk on the streets was less about the Civil War and more concerned with the internecine struggle between left-wing factions. The central authorities in Madrid's Cortes and Barcelona's Generalitat were every day cracking down more on revolutionist propaganda. In January 1937, the POUM's weekly newspaper was permanently suspended by the Madrid Defence Committee. On 10 February – the week before Ethel's broadcast above – the same authority seized POUM's Radio Madrid. Anarchist and Trotskyist printing presses were also confiscated. These acts of censorship were ordered and carried out by a government and committees in which sat CNT ministers – surely one of the few examples of ministers acting so brazenly against their own organisation and supporters. Of course, the anarchists were massively outnumbered at government level, and their predicament was precisely that which Emma Goldman had predicted. They were serving in a government increasingly at odds with their own aims.

Throughout February, disputes between communists and anarchists increased. On 15 February, the authorities in Valencia ordered the collection of all arms held by workers. The anarchist demand 'to arm the people' was going into reverse. Even amongst the militias, as Orwell reported in *Homage to Catalonia*, guns were hard to get hold of. In October of the previous year, the Republican government had formed the Popular Army, theoretically a united anti-fascist force. In reality, the various militias remained more or less independent. By early 1937 there was outright hostility in the official press and propaganda against the POUM and the combined CNT and FAI militias. Guns were issued to Popular Army officers but were refused to soldiers in the militias. POUM Combatants returning from the Aragon front were, according to Orwell, no longer celebrated and publicly thanked. Any credit for military successes was automatically attributed to the Republican Popular Army.

In Barcelona on 26 February the Generalitat outlawed public meetings across Catalonia. The revolutionary spirit of just a few weeks previously had all but gone. Expensive restaurants and shops re-opened, food prices rose and workers' wages dropped. People no longer addressed each other with *tú*, but the more formal and traditional *usted*. Workers' patrols were ordered to disband and the old pre-revolution police were out on the streets again instead. As the tension built, Ethel continued to broadcast. No doubt the anxieties of the time partially led to her tone of urgency, of people needing to act now.

The very concession that the anarchists had made six months previously was aggravating the situation. Despite Goldman's and others' warnings, many Spanish CNT and FAI leaders had argued vehemently that the CNT should be further represented in the Republican government.

'Since September 1936,' Professor Genovés explained, 'the leaders of the CNT and FAI felt that the disorder in Catalonia was excessive, and that they needed to make a more concerted effort of winning the war. Besides, the communists were calling them "uncontrollable savages", claiming that the war would be lost because of the anarchists. All of this made it clear to some within the movement that it was necessary to enter the government. First in the Catalan Generalitat, and then the Cortes in Madrid. But a radical minority was opposed from the beginning.'

Another Barcelona historian, Albert Barcells, agrees that, whether or not the anarchists were to blame for the alleged 'disorder', that was the perception. 'Anarchist leaders realised that the chaos, the assassinations in the rearguard, had to stop, and one way of doing that was to play a larger role in the government. This caused, in their own ranks, an enormous resistance to their leadership.'

The anarchists in the government were becoming every day more isolated, while the communist and socialist elements were increasingly convinced that they had to take action against the rank and file of the CNT and their allies. On 5 March 1937, the Communist Party congress called for the complete eradication of the Trotskyist POUM. By

April, the language of confrontation was shrill: a poster, designed by the Friends of Durruti, appeared on the streets of Barcelona, declaring, 'All power to the working class. All economic power to the unions. Instead of the Generalitat, the Revolutionary Junta!'

Jenny Patrick also broadcast from the CNT station. Although Ethel was the regular English-speaking voice, a great many people in Barcelona with an opinion to air were given access to the microphones. A talk Jenny gave on 29 March gives us an indication of the growing pessimism then. 'What do you think of the situation in Spain now?' she asked. 'Do you think that the revolution is progressing? For my part I see it slipping, slipping, and that has been the position for some time. However, perhaps it will be possible for it to be saved. Let us hope so, but it seems to me that reaction is gaining a stronger hold each day.'

The situation was made all the more volatile by the successes, and the violence, of the Nationalist generals' military advances. In early March the Italian corps took the important town of Guadalajara. At the end of the month a major offensive on the Basque Country began. In mid April Nationalist troops reached the Mediterranean and left Catalonia isolated from the rest of Republican territory. On 26 April, Guernica was bombed.

The Nationalist army, although powerful and highly organised on the ground, had very little air power. Nazi Germany, meanwhile, was anxious to test its air force. The Condor Legion was formed from within the Luftwaffe specifically to assist the Spanish generals. (It was spearheaded by Lieutenant von Richthofen, a cousin of World War I's Red Baron.)

Consequently, most of the Nationalist air power throughout the war was supplied by Hitler. The Condor Legion attacked Guernica late that Monday afternoon, low and in broad daylight, in the full knowledge that the city could offer no resistance. Guernica was utterly destroyed. Nearly 1,700 people were killed and another 1,000 injured. There was international outrage at the brutal and experimental attack, but the Nationalist leadership, in response, simply denied that the bombardment ever took place.

Throughout these months Ethel continued her broadcasts, as well as sending home her regular articles. But the revolutionary Barcelona she had loved and celebrated only had days to live. Orwell said of those last days of April that citizens mumbled among themselves, 'There's going to be trouble before long.' According to him, 'the danger was quite simple and intelligible.' He reported, too, that minor skirmishes between communists and anarchists throughout the region were becoming frequent, with CNT and UGT activists taking turns at assassinating one another. The anarchists have long claimed that some of the murders committed in their name were, in fact, the work of pro-communist agents provocateurs. A CNT member was murdered in April and thousands turned up on the streets in protest on the day of the funeral. On April 25, Roldán Cortada, an important member of the UGT, was assassinated. The communists organised an even greater demonstration at his funeral. The massed armed assault guards marched through anarchist districts, and the Popular Army was ordered to parade through the main streets. To Orwell's eyes, it was a communist show of strength.

'It is beyond any question,' Ethel said of the assassination of Cortada, 'that it was the act of an agent provocateur with the scheme in mind of destroying any possibility of unity between the CNT and the UGT. As the CNT has been and still is advocating unity between the two workers' syndicates, obviously this deed was perpetrated by some person or persons opposed to unity.'

May Day in Barcelona 1937 must count as one of the strangest in the history of that workers' celebration. The CNT had for months been working for a reconciliation with their UGT and PSUC counterparts. They urged a display of inter-party solidarity. But, on 30 March, the Generalitat, fearing a violent confrontation between factions, decided to call off all demonstrations. Barcelona – the epicentre of world radicalism, in a country actively fighting fascism – was the only city in Europe to have no workers' rally.

# 7

# The May Days

*∽ There is trouble in Barcelona! At 3 p.m. on May 3rd three lorry loads of police made use of the siesta hour to launch an attack on the telephone exchange. ∽*

With these words Ethel Macdonald began the most important commentary of her life, an on–the–spot reportage of events of historical importance and in which she herself was to play a perilous and telling role.

When Ethel first heard the news, she was sipping coffee with Jenny Patrick and some other colleagues. Only a few streets away, in a hotel lounge, another fighter for the cause heard the same piece of information. 'There's been some kind of trouble at the telephone exchange, I hear.' But George Orwell paid no attention at the time.

The PSUC and the government in the Generalitat had been perplexed for months by the CNT's control of the telephone exchange, or *telefónica*. On 1 May there had been the strange phenomenon of a revolutionary city with no May Day celebrations, and now two days later there was the

135

even stranger phenomenon of socialist armed guards, sent by the Catalan councillor for public order, Rodriguez Salas, to breach the offices of a fellow socialist organisation. Salas got *his* order directly from the Catalan minister for inner affairs, Antonio Ayguade, a communist. Workers against workers? Anti-fascists against anti-fascists? How could that be?

'Well, because the telephone exchange was very symbolic,' Mike Gonzalez explains. 'It was run by the workers, members of the CNT, and the government believed that they listened in on ministerial conversations. You can imagine what mayhem that could cause, if you actually heard what politicians say to each other! But more importantly, control of the *telefónica* was symbolic of the extent to which workers' organisations still controlled things in Barcelona.'

From an anarchist perspective, international concerns were uppermost in the minds of the Spanish Communist Party and the Republican government, both anxious to win the support of Britain and France. In order to win that support they had to demonstrate that the Spanish Civil War was *not* about revolution, but defending a bourgeois bureaucracy and nothing more. Sending troops against the workers was a demonstration to the outside world that the Republic would not allow a revolution to happen in Spain with all the consequent repercussions for the rest of Europe. On the day the exchange was attacked in Barcelona, so too were the exchanges in Tarragona and Tortosa, south of the city.

The truckloads of police and Guardia Alsalto (Assault Guards) took control of the ground floor of the exchange in Barcelona, but on the upper floors workers offered armed resistance. 'They seized the ground floor without difficulty,'

Ethel wrote, 'but our comrades in the building barricaded the stairways and swept them with machine-gun fire.

'Twelve of our comrades refused to allow this seizure to take place, and resisted. They were in the top part of the building, which faces directly onto the Plaza Catalunya. The Guardia Alsalto took up their positions in the bottom storey.'

According to Augustin Souchy – the anarchist comrade who had collected Ethel and Jenny in Perpignan five months earlier and introduced them to Barcelona –

> word of the assault spread in the square and, soon after, throughout the city. It was as though a match had been set to gunpowder. The workers of Barcelona, belonging to the CNT in an overwhelming majority, feared that this might be only the beginning of still further actions against their rights . . . Workers and police ran about excitedly in every section of the city. The union headquarters were full of people. Everybody wanted arms. Everybody wanted to be ready to defend other buildings from similar assaults. It was impossible to stem the indignation of the masses.

Ethel Macdonald was amongst those reacting to the extraordinary events:

> News reached Jenny and I as we were having coffee in a little anarchist restaurant not far from our headquarters in the Via Durruti. The messenger told us that three lorry loads of police had made use of the peaceful siesta hour, when shops and offices are closed, to launch their attack. Immediately, crowds gathered outside [the *telefónica*] and the streets were filled with men and women crying: 'To

137

the barricades! To the barricades!' It echoed throughout the streets and in a very short time firing had broken out all over the city.

The police had used sandbags and bricks intended to repel Franco's attack. Our anarchist comrades tore up loose paving stones to build their own barricades. There was electricity in the air . . .

She reported that rifle fire was coming from the street, and defensive fire from the upper-floor windows. 'Hurrying back to our headquarters, Jenny and I passed groups of men and women running, rifles in hand, to their appointed places behind the barricades or in the buildings that we controlled. The roar of traffic had died down and the only sounds were the heavy firing and the screaming of ambulances rushing to and from the hospitals.'

The city on that day was divided into two sides. On one, the Generalitat, the Socialist and Communist parties. On the other, the CNT, FAI and the POUM. Orwell felt that the POUM leaders tried not to get drawn into the conflict, but decided they had to defend their anarchist colleagues. Businesses immediately closed shop. Public transport was closed down. Trucks and cars filled with Popular Army soldiers, or militia men, careered wildly up and down Las Ramblas, the Barrio Gótico and the Raval, along all the major thoroughfares. Sporadic gunfire broke out in different areas across the town. Citizens scurried for safety. Confusion reigned throughout 3 May, many people unable to understand that it was their own Republican government had who ordered the attack.

Professor Genovés thinks that the causes of the situation

are more complicated than simply a communist–anarchist confrontation: 'The events of May can be considered as simply communist provocation. Provocation from the government which opposed the anarchists and their power. But there is also another way of assessing the events. The more radical minority of the CNT–FAI was opposed to its own leadership and collaboration with the government.' In other words, grassroots anarchists remained more radical than their leaders. Whatever the roots, Federica Montseny, García Oliver and other CNT ministers were unable to prevent the attack on their own movement.

The fighting continued throughout the rest of the day. People, if they were not directly involved, took refuge in CNT and POUM strongholds, such as the Hotel Falcon. 'Jenny and I went back to our hotel, the Oriente, that night. We had little difficulty, but we had to be very careful. We were stopped every few yards and searched for arms.'

In the evening, the Regional Committee of the CNT broadcast from their station that they were attempting to negotiate a withdrawal of the police from the *telefónica*. The armed workers held their fire and, for a moment, it seemed as if the crisis had been avoided. However, the Assault Guards and the police continued to disarm workers and militias, and fighting broke out again. 'All during the night there was firing in the street,' Jenny Patrick wrote. 'Ethel and I had a good view from the hotel windows.'

'The next morning we were preparing for attack,' Ethel wrote to Guy Aldred. On Tuesday 4 May, Lluís Companys, president of the Generalitat, until now a friend of the CNT, but increasingly under the control of the PSUC, requested that the authorities in Valencia provide aircraft to bomb the CNT barracks. The CNT, for their part, assembled militias and trained their guns on the palace of the Generalitat itself. Ethel and Jenny left their hotel, despite advice to remain inside.

Men barricaded windows; women dragged out cases of ammunition. Machine guns were mounted. We knew what was coming. I set out at seven. At that hour Spanish women go to the market. Both sides, knowing this, look out for them and cease fire to allow them to move about. [Jenny and I] mingled with these women, some of whom carried little white flags in their hands. We would slink along a street, hugging a wall. At every corner where we knew there was a barricade, one of the women would poke her little flag round. At this signal, firing would stop, and we would scurry across. Sometimes, though, firing went on above our heads and showers of plaster would fall about our ears. Behind every tree and every lamp post there was a soldier on one side or the other, and they would scowl at us, or smile, and wave us on.

In this way, we eventually reached the Via Durruti. We chatted with a comrade while waiting for a lull in the fighting. Five minutes later, we saw him fall.

Once inside we went up to the roof to see if we could see anything. As soon as we stuck our heads outside a burst of firing made us duck quickly and we had to crawl back to safety on our stomachs.

By this time it would have been impossible to put a nose into the Via Durruti. A little away from us was the police station. Looking at it from a sheltered window

we saw puffs of smoke coming out of every window
– for all the world like a wild and woolly west picture.
It was the same from another Government building on
our other side.

Jenny Patrick continued the story. 'The police were firing
from their building, and from nearby houses, and the
CNT were replying from inside their Headquarters at the
Telephone Exchange. The gunfire crossed from the balconies
over the Plaza Catalunya from the Colon Hotel, the Socialist
Party HQ . . . The noise is terrible! Already many have been
killed and wounded.'

At nine o'clock on that Tuesday night, the Generalitat
radio station issued an appeal from the leaders of the various
organisations – including García Oliver of the CNT – to
end the fighting It was ignored. Mariano Vasquez, secretary
of the CNT, made the broadcast:

> We must stop what is happening immediately so that
> our comrades at the front may face the enemy secure
> in the knowledge that they do not have to watch the
> rear because we cannot reach an agreement. Stop the
> shooting, comrades! But let no one try to win new
> positions when the firing has stopped. We shall continue
> our discussions here until we have found a solution. We
> have come together to seek a joint agreement because
> this fighting can only serve the purposes of our enemy.

Jenny Patrick claimed, in the *Barcelona Bulletin*, that the
provocation from the police continued anyway. 'A motor left
here yesterday afternoon, and it was stopped just up the road,

141

the occupants forced to alight. They were shot deliberately in cold blood . . . The Communist Party,' she concludes from this and similar events, 'is a menace to the workers in their struggle.'

'This was our life for the next three days,' Ethel reported.

> We busied ourselves filling cartridge clips for the soldiers and preparing meals for them . . . At meal times we felt that all the food we had was needed for them, and that we might try to have our meals in a little restaurant a few streets away which had remained open. It was funny to see the men lay down their arms, have their lunch, and start firing again . . . At the barricades we watched the soldiers and police drag easy chairs out of nearby buildings and sit, smoking, till it was time to start firing again. They seemed to take things as coolly as that.
>
> Sometimes we were able to take some food to them. We had to creep up to the barricades with it, crouching on the ground. If we had showed a head above, it would have been a signal for the firing to start.
>
> We could not get back to the hotel, so at nights we dragged mattresses under the windows of our rooms (the safest part of the rooms) and tried to get what sleep we could.
>
> If the Anarchists and Syndicalists do not take control now the workers of Spain will have gained nothing from all the fighting and loss of life.

That Wednesday, the Generalitat once again appealed for calm. The Regional Committee of the CNT announced a peace plan: 'Hostilities to cease. Every party to keep its positions.' The anarchists on the street, however, having been attacked, and feeling betrayed by their own leaders, were in no mood for calm. The police and factions of the Popular Army, for their part, seemed to be out of government control. The fighting intensified, focused in a few streets in the centre of the city.

'We saw twelve comrades dragged from their car and shot,' Ethel wrote. 'When the ambulance people tried to get to them they were ordered back and told if they went to these men they would be fired upon. Our comrades did not want to kill people and they withheld their fire as much as possible. They never attacked, contenting themselves with defence.'

By the evening of 5 May, and into the next day, while the gunfire continued, the fallout between the CNT membership on the streets and their representatives in government intensified.

On Thursday, the UGT and the CNT made a joint declaration. They broadcast it from all the various radio stations – including the CNT Barcelona Radio, which Ethel had not been allowed near during the fighting – and published it in every paper. 'All workers of the CNT and the UGT are ordered to return to work. All members of both trade unions should avoid anything that might lead to possible friction and disturbances at their place of work . . . Mutual understanding and solidarity are the requirements of the hour. To work, comrades of the CNT and UGT!'

The declaration was ignored. Workers did not return to their places of employment. The police continued their attacks.

'The ambulances are running about all the time. They ring a bell and collect all the wounded, of which, it is reported, there is an appalling amount.' By Friday, it was clear that the rank-and-file anarchists could not win out against the combined forces of the Generalitat, the police, the Assault Guards and their own ministers. Barricades were dismantled – but not those controlled by the PSUC, which would remain standing for some months to come as a warning against further resistance to the Republican government. There was talk of 'treachery' by the CNT leadership.

'Dead and wounded lay between the barricades,' Ethel reported of the end of the May Days. 'Wrecked cars were in every other street. Hardly a pane of glass was left in a window and all the street lamps were shattered. Walls were wrecked by bombs. Altogether 300 of our comrades were killed during those three days. I have no idea how many were wounded. As soon as the fighting stopped, wives and mothers hurried through the streets searching of their loved ones . . . The streets were filled with fear-stricken and frenzied women.'

Guy Aldred and John Taylor Caldwell sent Ethel and Jenny news reports of the week's events that had appeared in the British press. Jenny was outraged: 'The cuttings you sent all blamed the Anarchists for the trouble, but they were not in any way to blame. They have all the time adopted an attitude of conciliation and have compromised themselves almost out of existence in their eagerness to preserve anti-Fascist unity.'

Of course, compromising was part of the problem. The CNT representatives in the Generalitat were for more compromise than their foot soldiers were prepared to concede. Part of the problem was not simply a split in the left, but within the anarchist movement itself.

Ethel and Jenny summed up their thoughts on the entire week's events in articles printed in the *Barcelona Bulletin* in the middle of May.

> One point of view is that this provocation was deliberate, with the intention of splitting the anti-Fascist front and separating the Anarchists from all other sections. Our enemies wanted the struggle so that central Government could step in and crush the Anarchists completely . . . We may have lost men; we have lost the Telephone Exchange, *but our position is stronger normally.* No doubt there have been manoeuvres from outside Spain in this matter. [Have they] been the manoeuvres of England and France?

Noam Chomsky goes further: 'In fact, if you take a look at the Spanish Civil War, it had two phases. The first phase was a joint effort, in different ways, by fascists, communists and liberal democracies to crush this beast of freedom. People running their own lives, seeking freedom and justice – that can't be tolerated. So they all collaborated in crushing it. It was only after that was taken care of that they went to war on each other.'

This is more than a bold claim – that Britain, France and America essentially conspired with the Soviet Union and the Spanish Nationalists, and, by implication, with Nazi Germany and fascist Italy – to quash the Catalan anarchist revolution. Communists, democrats, and socialists would call the accusation an outrage; many thousands of non-anarchists gave up their lives in the name of anti-fascism. Even at a macro-political level, Chomsky's view is extreme on this matter.

'The point is,' Ethel ruminated, looking back on the May Days, 'were we wise in refusing to accept their challenge? Was not this the time to take over complete control? Would we necessarily have lost? We control the ammunition factories, the transport, practically all the means of sustenance. Would we have lost?'

Though she had been deeply anti-communist most of her political life, Ethel's tone after the May events became more hostile than ever. 'I do not think there is any solution except the elimination of the Communist Party . . . The petty bourgeoisie will be finished if their economic power is taken from them. But the Communist Party must be cleared out of everything, especially of the UGT and the Generalitat. The CNT must keep control of everything. They ought to have done this from the first.'

Once the fighting was over, the reprisals began. Augustin Souchy in *The Tragic Week in May* recalled the immediate aftermath:

> The following are names of comrades who were found murdered in various places outside the city: Mario Berruti, Baltasar Ballejo Mateo Freixas, Jose Gallisa, and Julian Martinez from Figueras . . . Many houses of our comrades have been searched. These searches were carried out by the police and members of the Communist and Catalan Nationalist Parties . . . After the airborne troops had retired, assault guards and members of the Communist and Catalan Nationalist Parties invaded the headquarters of the CNT. They forced the doors open and destroyed the furniture. Thefts were committed in all the CNT local branches.

On May 9th, a mysterious ambulance left twelve terribly mutilated bodies on the road between Bella Terra and Sardanola Ripolet. The corpses were identified as those of the twelve young Anarchists from Armonia del Palomar. These are the names of some of them: Cesar, Fernandez Nari, Jose Villena, Juan Antonio y Luis Carnera.

In order to stop the fighting the various organisations had agreed upon a pact, which included the immediate release of prisoners held by both sides. According to Souchy, the CNT and the FAI remained true to their word.

They were self-disciplined and immediately released hundreds of prisoners, most of whom had put themselves under the protection of the Anarchists voluntarily. Their opponents were not so faithful to their promises. Long negotiations were required before the Communists and the Catalan Nationalists would release their Anarchist prisoners. A full week after the re-establishment of normality, many members of the CNT and the FAI were still being held.

The revolution in Catalonia was definitively over.

Ethel herself was not, at this stage, one of the anarchist activists arrested and taken away. She presumed that her British citizenship provided her with a certain amount of protection. If part of the May Days assault was to calm the parliament's nerves over revolution, then neither the Communist Party nor the Generalitat would be keen to arrest Britons, whether they were anarchists or not.

Jenny Patrick left for Madrid. It had always been part of their programme that Jenny would travel beyond Barcelona, and get closer to the overall state power in the capital. Money had always been tight for the two Scottish women – now it was virtually non-existent. Comrades in Madrid would be able to help, and it was important to bring news of the terrible events in Barcelona to them. Jenny Patrick would only stay there for a week. She was back in Glasgow at the end of May, informing the British public of the revolution's betrayal – and the difficult position Ethel Macdonald now found herself in. Meanwhile, Ethel remained free, but discovered that her name *had* been put on a government black list.

'The immediate effect of my appearance on the black list was very disconcerting. My supply of money from home died away. I had been getting it regularly but now did not receive a farthing. There was nothing for it but to throw myself on the mercy of the CNT. They themselves were not too well off.'

Worse than the financial situation – a predicament Ethel was well used to by this time in her life, and one shared by the majority of her comrades – was the enforced isolation. Her broadcasting days were over; in the new politics of Barcelona a voice like Ethel's was no longer tolerated. On her eventual return to Scotland, she would write a series of articles telling the story of those difficult months in Spain. 'Not only money, but letters stopped coming through. I knew that many were actually sent from home, but they never reached me.'

Being free was not without its psychological pressure

148

either. 'Why did they not arrest me and be done with it! I could not make that out. Later, I learned that they had already arrested so many British subjects that they were afraid to arrest more.'

Ethel used the situation constructively. 'I was free. Apart from making representations to the authorities – who hated me – on behalf of other prisoners, I had little to do. Sometimes I would spend an hour or two in a café with some of the comrades.'

If they hated her already, it took some courage to make herself so plainly visible, and a thorn in the authorities' side. We should remember that from the middle of May on into the summer, not only were anarchists being arrested, but killed. It would have been quite easy – in fact, perhaps the simplest solution – for elements in the government to explain Ethel Macdonald's 'disappearance' on 'savage' members of the disorderly extreme left. Nevertheless, Ethel continued with what she saw as her duty.

'On several occasions the Assault Guards raided the café looking for armed revolutionaries. I passed myself off as a wife of one or other of the men. By simply not talking, I managed to bluff them. It was nerve-wracking . . . On one occasion a young lad slipped me two bombs and a kind of blackjack. I put the bombs in my pocket and sat on the jack . . . The guards searched everyone – but missed me.'

As was so typical of Ethel all her life, in this series of articles she prefers to speak of others rather than herself – despite the dangerous work she was carrying out on a daily basis. The people she met in the early summer of 1937 give us a picture of life in immediately post-revolutionary Barcelona.

Throughout the May Days, Jenny and Ethel were often in the company of their friend Charlie Doran, who had recently been fighting alongside Orwell in the POUM. 'Charlie lived in Earl Street, Scotstoun before he came to Spain. He decided that his duty lay with the Spanish workers just about a week after he was married. Charlie was enamoured of Barcelona and told us that, when the Civil War was over, he intended to settle there and send for his wife . . . Actually he did return to this country – but it was because he was shocked by the death of Bob Smillie, and the manner in which the POUM was being persecuted.'

Smillie was the grandson of Robert Smillie, socialist, miners' leader, and MP until 1929. Charlie had returned to Spain to add his weight and influence to the Republican cause and to the brigades as a fighting soldier. Ethel wrote, in a prescient letter to Guy Aldred: 'Poor Smillie! He looks as if he were jailed for life – or death. For they will never let him back to Britain alive with the facts he has collected against the Communist Party, its activities and alliances in Spain.'

The circumstances of Smillie's death in Valencia in 1937 have been the cause of much bitter argument ever since. It was claimed that he was kicked to death by his communist interrogators, a view which George Orwell shared.

David Murray, the Motherwell ILP journalist, disagreed. Bob Smillie had been arrested for not having the necessary papers on his way home from Spain in May 1937. He was taken to prison in Valencia where the charges against him grew. The ILP sent the fluent Spanish-speaking Murray to assist him. In early June Smillie began to feel stomach pains which were attributed, much too late, to appendicitis. He died, according to Murray's account, in hospital of peritonitis. Murray was in Valencia at the time, in touch with Smillie himself, as well as the Republican authorities. Yet other versions of the ILP volunteer's demise persist to this day. Murray held Ethel Macdonald at least partially responsible for this. 'She claimed to have special knowledge about Bob Smillie,' he later said, 'and continued to spread the story that he was done to death.' But it wasn't only Ethel who was suspicious of the circumstances. Bob's own father ultimately believed that Murray was hiding something. Georges Kopp, the Belgian commander of the POUM unit Smillie had fought for, insisted he saw official documents that proved Smillie had been kicked and beaten to death. Ethel supported this view, claiming inside knowledge that the secret police had murdered the Scots Poumista. David Murray continued to repudiate her claims, claiming that her story was 'full of errors'. Although there are grey areas in Murray's own account (*Homage To Caledonia* discusses them in depth) it is hard to know why Murray, an ILP man, outspoken over the Republic's treatment of POUM prisoners and often supportive of the anarchists, should have lied.

Another old friend she met was Dan Mullen from Victoria Crescent, Blantyre. 'Dan stood six foot three in his socks. My first sight of him in Barcelona was his tall figure lying in a hospital bed with both his legs stretched up in the air and weights attached to each . . . Dan had been wounded severely [by the Assault Guards]. One leg was broken and bullets entered his other foot and one arm.'

Ethel also ran into James Maxton, a friend and follower of James McLean, the two of them legendary 'Red Clydesiders'.

A Member of Parliament for the ILP, he had broken with the Labour Party, deeply opposed to its reactionary policies in the aftermath of the General Strike. It was Maxton who spearheaded the ILP's split as a whole from Labour.

'He was in Spain to make some inquiries regarding the POUM persecutions, but he was very worried all the time about his wife. "I'm not getting letters from her," he told me. I told him not to worry. Letters came through very irregularly, but I know this comfort did not satisfy him.

'All this time I kept up my regular visits to comrades in prison. Some of them had been removed to the Hotel Falcon because Maup Stevens had written to the authorities on behalf of all the other prisoners, complaining that the conditions under which they were living were terribly bad.'

Maup Stevens was a Dutch anarchist friend of Ethel's whom, eventually, Ethel would help get out of prison and escape Spain.

Stevens was only one of many Ethel helped. Acting as a kind of unofficial escape officer was what Ethel felt was the best use of her time, still being on the 'outside'. She smuggled food and letters into the makeshift prisons, helping in particular any non-Spanish nationals, far from home and family, like herself. She brought a constant source of information in, and took messages out. She made it her business to find connections at the port and with the French border to the north – the only routes through which international volunteers could leave Spain.

Ethel begged, stole, or borrowed clothes and had them ready for any released prisoners. Without papers, and still dressed either in militia uniforms or prison duds, they would have had no hope of leaving the country legally. Worse, they could be re-arrested. She spoke to the captains and crews of foreign ships and organised safe passage for her comrades – or at least as safe as was humanly possible. In essence, Ethel was engaged in resistance work, and in broad daylight, with Assault Guards on every corner.

She was no longer a journalist. Denied access to microphones and finding it ever more difficult to get articles out of the country, she found another role. Instead of writing about the revolution she was actively engaged in its defence. If she was in danger before, she increased the peril for herself tenfold. She was an activist first and foremost, and when action was required of her, she did not flinch.

'About this time,' Ethel wrote, 'I was becoming more and more sure that I would soon be among those prisoners. It is necessary to have a permit to remain in Spain for more than three months.' Ethel had been there now for seven. 'My permit had expired and I did not renew it. If I had tried to renew it late, I would have been in the soup. Without it, I was also in the soup. It seemed to be just a matter of time before I was roped in.

'One night, about eleven o'clock, when I had just finished cleaning out my room, there was a thunderous knocking at the door.'

# 8

# *The Scots Scarlet Pimpernel*

～ *Our victory is sure because the Spanish proletariat have the will to conquer! The superhuman determination of the workers that destroyed the whole Fascist army in Catalonia will be repeated in Andalusia and Aragon. For five months Madrid, the brave capital of Revolution, has demonstrated that it is invincible.* ～

From the middle of May onwards as many as 3,500 anarchists were incarcerated in prisons and work camps throughout Catalonia. The very people who, only days before, had effectively run the city, who had brought about a revolution of the most profound kind and maintained it for months, were now rounded up by the government they had fought for and for which many of their comrades had died. Despite the anarchist representatives staying on in the Generalitat for several months, the Catalan Nationalists and communists were safely in control. All those who had fought against them during the May Days were in danger. The leaders and activists of POUM were jailed, and sometimes killed, alongside their anarchist comrades.

Andres – or Andreu in Catalan – Nin was one of the founders of the POUM, and entered the Republican government as councillor of justice. But in June he and the rest of the POUM leadership were arrested and transported to a prison camp in Alcalá de Henares near Madrid. Only later did it come to light that most of them were executed, including Nin, on 20 June.

'On 15 June,' Orwell wrote, 'the police suddenly arrested Andres Nin in his office, and the same evening raided the Hotel Falcon and arrested all the people in it, mostly militiamen on leave. The place was converted immediately into a prison, and in a very little while it was filled to the brim with prisoners of all kinds. Next day the POUM was declared an illegal organisation and all its offices, book-stalls, sanatoria, Red Aid centres and so forth were seized . . . As early as 21 June the rumour reached Barcelona that he [Nin] had been shot.'

Ethel wrote of the murder: 'Despite theories to the contrary and despite statements made by alleged responsible persons there exists no doubt in Barcelona that Nin is dead, murdered by the agents of Stalinism.' She reported in the British press later: 'It was publicly stated by Federica Montseny at a huge meeting held in Barcelona that the bodies of Nin and two other persons had been discovered in Valencia on the road.' Nin himself had been tortured before dying.

Accusations that Nin had 'never worked' because he had 'always been in the pay of Hitler' were common, as was the allegation that POUM and the anarchists were counter-revolutionaries working directly for the fascists and were secretly supporters of Franco and the Nationalists. Ethel Macdonald would soon come to know the allegation only too well.

It is now known that two of Nin's assassins were members of the Soviet secret police. As Professor Genovés put it, 'Stalinist purges were being exported to Barcelona.'

In the country at large, the Nationalist army continued to make progress. On 12 June a campaign to take Republican Bilbao began, the army breaking through the city's 'Iron Ring' defences, and the Condor Legion attacking from the air. A week later the fascists won the city. The war generally was going badly. The Government depended more and more on arms from the Soviet Union. The whole of the Republic became militarised – including the Law, which became arbitrary in the extreme. Thousands of people ended up imprisoned under a new kind of undeclared martial law, without due process or fair trial.

Had Ethel chosen to lie low, perhaps smuggling herself quietly out of the country, that knock on the door might never have come about. But she had remained active; helping others escape and delivering mail and goods to prisoners was never going to make the authorities forget her.

'Three Assault Guards marched in. Without a word of explanation they started to ransack every corner and every cupboard. My personal belongings were strewn about the floor.

'They found my journalist's card, endorsed by the CNT and recognised by the Government. And they found enough revolutionary literature to hang me.'

The collection of newspapers, posters and articles that

Guy Aldred and Ethel donated years later to Glasgow's Mitchell Library is indicative of the kind of documents they were likely to have found: the CNT daily newspaper; FAI leaflets; other anarchist journals from Barcelona, Madrid and France; replies to Ethel's letters from Guy, John Taylor Caldwell, and fellow anarchists. In other words, the kind of material that, until several weeks earlier, had been circulating freely in every bar, pinned on lampposts in every street. Much of it, naturally, would have been fiercely critical of the Communist Party and the Soviet Union.

'Some time previously I had been ill, in hospital. When I was discharged the nurse visited me to give me some injections.'

As far as I can discover this is the only reference Ethel makes to being ill during her stay in Barcelona; nothing else is mentioned in any of the many letters, articles, speeches and broadcasts she made. It tells us two things: firstly, that she was strong, and private. We know now of the trauma she went through with her neglectful lover many years before and the loss of her child – which was never to be mentioned again. She lived with, and contained, her personal difficulties, without recourse to others. Secondly, this off-the-cuff remark about being sick in Barcelona reminds us that Ethel was a profoundly communitarian character. *Her* life, *her* story, was not the story she was interested in, or wanted us to take an interest in, except as a minor detail in the great scheme of things. Although an impassioned speaker and writer, she saw herself as part of a community, a movement, nothing more.

Of the medicines found in her rooms, she says: 'The Guards were suspicious and held a conference over them.'

Perhaps the Assault Guards discovered what they were and what was ailing Ethel. We never do.

> They demanded to see my passport. On this being shown they informed me that I was in Spain illegally – although I had entered Spain before the barrier was erected at the border against foreigners. Then they tried to make me admit that I was French and wanted to leave the country with money. Proofs to the contrary were useless. They believed what they wanted to believe.
>
> Finally I was taken with five other comrades to an office of the Public Order Delegation. All papers and documents were taken, and all protests were met with the reply that if we were true anti-Fascists we would not object to our stuff being searched and ourselves questioned. The whole proceeding [at the Delegation] was absurd.
>
> After questioning, two of the comrades were released, but the rest of us were transferred to a police station for the night. The three male comrades were placed in an underground cell, but I, being a woman, was permitted to stay upstairs, where I had to pass the night sleeping on a chair.
>
> [The police] wanted me to sign some document or other, but I refused. Partly because it was in Spanish and partly because I was in a bad temper.

While she was not an individualist, Ethel's reportage is human. The individual – including herself – is part of every story. That line about being in a 'bad temper' is not only wry, but brings the reader into the situation. She was one of many men and women rounded up, questioned, imprisoned, maltreated. We can imagine that most of them were in a bad mood.

'The following evening our friends from the Public Order Delegation came again to ask us to sign a paper to the effect that we had been arrested for not having our [own] papers in order. I might add that two of the comrades had just five days ago returned from the front and had all their papers in order. Although, naturally, they had no passports, being Germans who had been expelled from their country.'

From the Delegation building, Ethel and her co-accused were taken back to the police station in the Via Durruti – a street name that must have struck them all as suddenly incongruous.

'From the police station I was removed to the Hotel Falcon in a motor lorry – for all the world like a tumbrel of the French Revolution.'

Being imprisoned in the Hotel Falcon, only a fortnight before the headquarters of the POUM, was bitter irony. This was where George Orwell had been a frequent visitor, and it was the centre of operations he headed to immediately when fighting broke out on 5 May. Had he and Ethel ever brushed past one another, or shared a conversation, it would have been in the Falcon. The POUM militia had, ironically, benefited from fighting on the Aragon front – at least they were out of the way of the hostilities in Barcelona. Soon after the May Days, Orwell returned to what many POUM members must have thought of as the relative safety of the battleground. Not for Orwell himself – he was wounded in the throat by a sniper bullet. (He had been warned often enough by comrades and friends about his cavalier attitude to, in this case literally, sticking his head over the parapet.) He and Ethel would never meet now.

When he returned to the city, suffering badly from the wound, Orwell found Barcelona unrecognisable. 'Over the POUM buildings the red flags had been torn down, Republican flags were floating in their place, and knots of armed Assault Guards were lounging in the doorways . . . The POUM bookstalls had been emptied of books and the notice-board further down Las Ramblas had been plastered with an anti-POUM cartoon.'

Ethel's comparison with the French Revolution is unavoidable. During the Reign of Terror, rival factions turned upon each other and the ultimately victorious, led initially by Robespierre, ruthlessly exterminated all potential enemies. Thoughts of the guillotine could not have been far from Ethel's mind given the amount of anarchists who were found dead on the streets. She might also have thought about Buonaparte – revolutions that result in the creation of a dictatorial regime.

'Once inside the Hotel Falcon which was to be my prison, I set about making myself at home . . . I was *incommunicado*. That is, I was not allowed to see or talk to anyone.'

However, the next morning Ethel realised that her window overlooked a backyard in which the male prisoners were allowed a little time to exercise. 'So I was soon deep in conversation with all the people to whom I had previously been bringing food.'

And soon, too, she would be finding a proactive use of her time in prison.

'Five days later my fingerprints were taken, but no charge

had been preferred against me.' And she adds, in that stalwart manner of hers, 'I set about making myself at home.'

Back in Scotland, according to Ethel's nephew Freddie Turrell, her family still had no idea that she was in Spain. Articles over the last seven months, both by and about her, had appeared in the *Evening Times*, the *Bellshill Speaker* and national newspapers. It's strange that her family missed all of them – wouldn't her family have been looking out for her articles? Most writers experience something similar; after a while family and close friends get used to their profession and take little notice. It is also possible that Andrew and Daisy and the rest of the Macdonald clan knew Ethel was writing about the Spanish Civil War – wasn't everyone? – without realising she was actually *there*. What is surprising is that none of them heard any of her radio broadcasts. Given that there would soon be an outcry in Britain about their sudden cessation and that even listeners in America worried, the fact that Ethel's own family was unaware of her broadcasting fame is all the more inexplicable.

Although those months must have been the longest period in which Ethel was out of touch with her family, she had been so for protracted periods before and would be again. John Taylor Caldwell barely knew any of her family and Guy Aldred was never likely to contact Ethel's parents – Daisy had made plain her dislike of him. The fact is that Ethel's family were blissfully unaware of her situation. They would soon find out, though, and not in the most pleasant of ways.

Ethel Macdonald's articles detailing the story of her

161

arrest and imprisonment did not appear until September. 'In Scotland, the group to which I am attached has always been in complete opposition to the Communist Party,' she wrote in a piece for the *Evening Times* on the 27th of that month. 'In opposing their propaganda we have always had to face and deal with their fundamental ignorance and brutality.'

The group to which Ethel was attached was, of course, Guy's United Socialist Movement. That it had 'always' been anti-communist is an understandable simplification. We know how Guy reacted to events almost spontaneously. By the time he formed the USM, however, any patience he had had with the Communist Party had run out. Certainly in the time since Ethel had joined forces with him, they had no truck with communism. 'My arrest was typical of the attitude of the Communist Party . . . In Spain, despite the fact that the membership of the party is made up of quite a different class to that in Britain, their approach is the same. Given the least little power they answer the arguments of their opponents with force.'

That notion, that Spanish rank-and-file communists are 'different' to their British comrades, is a point Ethel makes several times, without ever quite defining what she means. Certainly, the PCE (Partido Comunista Español) was much larger than its British counterpart. In Ethel's experience in Scotland, the Communist Party drew support almost exclusively from the working class; in Spain the demographic was much wider, with more middle- and upper-middle-class card-carriers. For Ethel, that was a problem: the party's instincts became more petit bourgeois, less radical, more obedient.

In the Hotel Falcon Ethel found herself locked up alongside volunteers who had been fighting with the POUM
militia.

> The spirit of the comrades in prison is good. Persecution
> and imprisonment of revolutionists is not something
> new to Spain, and many of the foreign comrades have
> suffered similar treatment in their respective countries...
>
> Persecution by so-called Communists ... is not new.
> The treatment meted out to revolutionaries in Russia
> today beggars description ... But that in Spain whilst
> their comrades and brothers are struggling at the fronts
> against the Fascist enemy, that revolutionists should be
> arrested on such a scale is a scandal that brings discredit
> on all those who permit it to take place without making
> protest. Revolution should mean the end of prisons, not
> the changing of the prison guards.

Ethel was very aware of the particular dangers facing
German and Italian volunteers for the Republic – their own
compatriots, in far greater numbers, were fighting them on
the ground and in the air in Spain, with the backing of their
governments and with more and better weapons.

> [Their] plight in Spain is pathetic. Expelled from
> Germany and Italy, they found refuge in France and
> other countries. But with the Spanish revolution they
> gave up what little they had in order to help in the great
> fight. But today, thanks to the counter-revolutionary
> Communist Party, they are destitute. Hundreds in
> prison, others expelled from Spain with no possibility

of security in any other country. In Spain itself they are liable to arrest at any moment. As the reaction advances, more and more of them will be arrested and expelled.

What happens to our arrested comrades we cannot tell. Where are they? No information is permitted to reach the public because of the strict censorship of the press. Anything could happen to them.

If inquiries are made regarding persons who have gone missing no satisfaction is obtained. They may be in prison, they might be dead. We have no means of knowing. Like Nin, they may be murdered.

The extreme arbitrariness of an unofficial martial law affected foreign prisoners even more harshly than Spanish nationals. 'The process was called "photo booth" or quick and expeditious justice,' says Professor Genovés. 'Very many people ended up in prisons and work camps where even the minimum procedural and legal guarantees were ignored.'

Ethel's on-the-spot view of the lack of judicial process testified to that.

No opportunity is given to persons once arrested to collect their personal goods before leaving the country . . . Evidently it is concluded that once a person is arrested he will have no further use for civilian clothes.

The following case is but one of many: the wife of a German comrade visited him in prison twice weekly. This comrade had been arrested when he came from the front on a special mission. He was transferred to the house of detention in the Calle Angel, where the Cheka is situated. [The wife] was given permission to bring him a blanket and food, but although she set out to take these to him, she has not been seen since. Obviously it was merely a trick to arrest her too.

Ethel writes 'Cheka' but the term used in Spanish at the time was *checas*. The political police were so-called after their Soviet model; they were, after all, introduced to Republican Spain by the Communist Party, organised by, in many cases, Soviet advisors. As many as 12,000 people may have been killed in these secret *checas* common throughout the Republican-held areas; although given that such claims have been made by right-wing anti-Republicans during and after the Franco era, more research may be required.

'And the persecution goes further,' Ethel wrote. 'It reaches out to the foreign correspondents of newspapers.

'The correspondent for the largest Liberal paper in Britain has been missing for five weeks. No information can be obtained regarding him despite the intervention of two consuls. This man is not British but Italian and, I understand, acted merely as the correspondent of his paper and took no active part in any political affairs of Spain.

'Arrested persons,' Ethel concluded, 'have absolutely no protection whatsoever and are completely under the control of the authorities.'

Anyone in such a situation would have been dismayed and frightened. For a lifelong anarchist it was more than just a vindication of her suspicion of authority in general; it was anathema to her spirit, to everything she fought for and struggled against. The flaunting of basic human rights and legal processes shocked Ethel. 'According to Spanish law a person can be kept "*incommunicado*" for five days and must have a charge laid against him within 30 days or be released. This does not operate in practice. Comrades are placed in a cell and allowed no visitors for as long as the authorities wish. The length of their detention without trial is likewise. The cases are too numerous to cite of prisoners kept for months without communication and without trial.'

The conditions under which prisoners were kept would soon come to light – partly as a result of Ethel Macdonald's own case. But she was one of the first to let the outside world know of the shortcomings of the premises used for incarceration and the abuses detainees were subject to.

The general sanitary condition of Barcelona leaves much to be desired. The conditions in which comrades in prison lived, particularly during the first weeks of the wholesale arrests, are nearly beyond description.

The police stations and the prisons were so full that garages and shops were used as detention houses. In one of these garages, next door to the police headquarters in the Via Durruti, 140 comrades were kept. Those who were fortunate had a blanket to sleep on, but the majority were compelled to sleep upon the stone floor. This was not solely for one night, but for weeks, and in some cases months.

For these 140 men there was one toilet and one lavatory. And the food! Twice a day a plate of soup, consisting of rice and potatoes.

In the Hotel Falcon I saw many men from the International Brigade who were weak physically through this enforced diet. Being foreigners and having no friends in Barcelona they had no means of obtaining anything else.

These are the men who, weeks or months previously, had given up jobs, left families and put any money they might have had into travelling to a foreign country to fight in a foreign war – because they believed their cause was just. Now the Republic they had risked their lives for was treating them appallingly.

David Murray echoed Ethel's description of Communist Party abuses:

> I saw Communist Party prisoners in jail with nothing else but their jackets and bags, for four or five months, not a shirt or a pair of underpants. I have been very disappointed with the Communist Party both here and in Spain. They seem to have a craze for publicity, and necessary jobs which bring no aura of glory are left undone. All the leaders want to be big shots and they have an enormous capacity for venomous insult.

The absence of Ethel's voice on the radio and the disappearance of her name from the newspapers and bulletins she wrote for caused a great deal of concern back home. The Anti-Parliamentary Communist Federation announced that 'considerable anxiety regarding [Ethel Macdonald's] welfare [was] felt by her relatives and comrades in Glasgow'. Interestingly, it was the A-PCF itself who formed The Ethel Macdonald Defence Committee. The USM, of course, joined them, but given the arguments prior to Ethel's and Jenny's departure, we can only assume that, Jenny Patrick herself, who had returned to Glasgow on 24 May, had built bridges and was the moving force behind the committee. The Anti-Parliamentarians had lost their premises at that time, and used those of the USM, so the two groups were working together, tentatively at least, again.

The British press dubbed Ethel 'the Scots Scarlet Pimpernel'. News of how she had helped prisoners and those hiding from the authorities escape had filtered through. Sub-editors quickly made the connection with Baroness Orczy's hero. Ethel, once she read the articles for herself, must have baulked at the comparison. Helping aristocrats escape revolutionaries? Hardly. Newspapers headlined stories about the 'Bellshill Girl Anarchist' (though Ethel was 28 at the time), demanding to know her whereabouts and the state of her health. Readers' letters were sent to editors of American papers. Eventually, questions were asked in the British parliament. Ethel had become the embodiment of all the British volunteers rounded up and silenced by the Republican authorities.

Freddie Turrell heard the story of how the family found out. 'A journalist from the *Bellshill Speaker* arrived at their door one day. He told them that Ethel was being held in a prison in Spain.'

They didn't believe him. They still did not know that Ethel had even gone to Barcelona. The journalist had to convince them, and when at last he did, Daisy and Andrew and Ethel's younger siblings still living at home were horrified. 'My grandmother, in a bit of a state,' Freddie says, 'told the journalist at one point that she'd sell anything in her house to raise whatever money she could if it would help her daughter.'

The *Evening Times* printed the comment the following day (2 August) and for the rest of that week, as if the shock of the news about Ethel wasn't bad enough, the Macdonald family had strangers knocking on their door at all hours of the day trying to buy their furniture and belongings.

Andrew and Daisy went to see the British consul and spoke to everyone they hoped might be able to help. The combined efforts of the Macdonald family and the A–PCF/ USM, together with the press interest, made the matter ever more urgent for the British government. In June 1937, a senior figure in the Labour movement, Fenner Brockway, went to Spain with the government's blessing. His mission was to discover what had happened to British subjects who had been detained.

∼

Archibald Fenner Brockway was a protégé of James Keir Hardie, who had turned him from being a youthful liberal into a socialist. He joined the ILP and edited the *Labour Elector* newspaper. Like Guy Aldred, Brockway's pacifism led him to oppose World War I, for which he served time in prison. Brockway and Aldred knew each other from shared correspondence and speaking on the same platforms. They had their differences – the former a socialist, the latter more libertarian and revolutionary – but also coincided over many issues, including India and women's rights.

Brockway's commitment to pacifism changed when he saw the threat of fascism in Germany, Italy and Spain – and, indeed, in Great Britain. He resigned from War Resisters' International, saying,

If I were in Spain at this moment I should be fighting with the workers against the Fascist forces. I believe it to be the correct course to demand that the workers shall be provided with the arms which are being sent so freely by the Fascist powers to their enemies. I appreciate the attitude of the pacifists in Spain who, whilst wishing the workers success, feel that they must express their support in constructive social service alone. My difficulty about that attitude is that if anyone wishes the workers to be triumphant he cannot, in my view, refrain from doing whatever is necessary to enable that triumph to take place.

Brockway became an important conduit for volunteers, including Orwell, who wished to go to Spain.

In 1929 Brockway had been elected to Parliament for the Labour Party (neither of which would have pleased Guy) but subsequently bitterly opposed Ramsay MacDonald's National Government. He returned to the ILP and, in 1937, was its general secretary. It was in this capacity that he went to Spain, with the acknowledged blessing of the government, albeit tacit – its policy of non-intervention made it difficult for it to intercede directly, and the *brigadistas* after all were breaking the law by fighting for the Republic. Brockway made it clear that although he intended to help Ethel, he was not party to many of her political beliefs: 'She is an anarchist and has no connection with our party [the ILP].'

Brockway visited Ethel and others at the Falcon, where he found a 'grotesque scene', according to Professor Genovés. 'A hundred and fifty people packed tightly together, with only one toilet and one sink between them. And with very little food.' No vestige of its former use as the headquarters for the CNT could be seen, much less so anything of the hotel it originally was.

Professor Genovés claims that she found some of Brockway's reports in Moscow. 'Which means that this leader of the international labour movement must have sent reports to London, but they were intercepted by Soviet agents.' The *checas* were clearly operating skilfully in Barcelona and Valencia.

By the end of June, Ethel was insisting that she be formally charged. Without knowing the accusations against her she had no hope of fighting them. At no point did the authorities ever make their accusations directly to Ethel. Fenner Brockway insisted that he be told the charges, and eventually he was. It was he who informed Ethel later of what she stood accused. Even if she had been given the opportunity to speak against her indictments she would have found it difficult, as they were a bizarre mix of distorted facts and outright falsehoods:

- She was found to be in possession of foreign money. (This was clearly true: Ethel had kept some francs and British pounds aside for her eventual return to Scotland.)

- She was in possession of revolutionary literature. (As was nearly every citizen of Barcelona at the time, that literature being from the CNT, the FAI and their international sister organisations.)

- Her passport was not in order. (Ethel rejected this accusation, and was later found to be in the right. Her passport – though not her visa and travelling papers – was up to date.)

- The other accusations were more serious and problematic:

- She had 'associated with prisoners'.

- She had 'conspired with them, and in a foreign tongue'.

- She was in possession of fascist literature.

The first two of these accusations were really one, and referred to her assistance of prisoners prior to her arrest – bringing clothes and food, smuggling in letters, and so on. Ethel's Spanish had never become fluent, and in any case she saw her duty as helping the international volunteers to whom she could only have spoken in English.

The charge of possessing fascist literature was the most dangerous – especially as Ethel admitted to it. 'The accusation that I was a Fascist,' she wrote, was based on 'files in my possession that had formerly belonged to a Fascist. In fact, I had found them in the CNT building and merely made use of them.' Ethel was a journalist, and it was her duty to know what the Nationalists, and their allies in Germany and Italy, were doing. No political organisation is without information on the opposition. Her articles and speeches refer constantly to Nationalist aims and strategies, information she could only locate in their own publications. Still, given the authorities' tactic of staining all anarchists with 'counter-revolutionary' tendencies, the accusation was a grave one.

Still ignorant of the charges against her, and unaware of the efforts being made on her behalf both abroad and in Spain by Fenner Brockway, Ethel had no choice but to carry on with daily life in her makeshift prison. Far from playing safe or keeping a low profile until she knew what she was fighting, she redoubled her efforts on behalf of her fellow inmates.

> I was always a thorn in the flesh of the Barcelona authorities. In prison, I was no better. I started to engineer ways and means of smuggling out letters about the prisoners and what was happening to them.
>
> I used to collect packets of letters from the other prisoners and smuggle them out with my own – in the cans in which my food had been brought into prison. Several persons brought in my food – but none of them knew they were taking out letters!
>
> The cans – thanks to careful planning – always landed in the hands of the same man, and he knew what to do with them. Those for abroad were handed to a French skipper, and those for the British Consul . . . reached him.

The resistance-style work she had done at the ports before her arrest was continuing to pay off. On the face of it, there is an agreeable Ealing-comedy innocence in Ethel's light-hearted telling of the story. But it must have taken real courage. Here is an Ethel we have not met before. We know she was practical and organised in her personal life. She had been a manager in her time, and had helped bring some order to the USM's office. But smuggling letters in food cans to 'fences' on the outside and ensuring their eventual delivery to foreign boats and consulates is of a higher order of organisational acumen.

> By means of this channel too, we managed to organise a hunger strike in every prison in Barcelona in which

there were Anarchist prisoners. Food was bad – potatoes and rice and a slice of bread twice a day. We were not satisfied in a host of small ways.

It was the same in other prisons and we persuaded them all to strike at a certain hour of a certain day.

Since the dawn of her political life Ethel had been a political provocateuse, a rabble-rouser; but until now she had done so with words, one step away from active resistance. In prison, she was in the thick of it, making things happen, and often doing so alone: 'We tried to get the CNT to support us with publicity, but they refused on the principle that we would only make things worse for ourselves.'

The scorn in Ethel's voice comes across loud and clear in that final sentence. Ethel was always for taking an opponent on face to face. In that sense she was no politician – compromise and casuistry were not part of her make-up. Where there was an injustice, a crime, it should be condemned and righted forthwith and without conditions.

'You can be sure that I spent my time arranging how, when one of us got out, we would help the others to flee the country. Everything was cut and dried. Street plans were prepared and everyone knew exactly what to do and where to go.'

All this in crowded conditions, underfed, and recovering from illness – and under the noses of her captors. 'I am alive. And prepared to risk everything in order to be alive. From small effort comes the great struggle . . .'

# 9

# *Escape*

*∽ Madrid calls. Barcelona calls. Your past calls. Workers of Britain − act! ∽*

'What of our comrades without friends and without a country? Are they to be permitted to rot in prison because we are not prepared to help them? Brave comrades who have already suffered too much persecution and imprisonment are lying in Spanish jails for no other crime than having in revolutionary Spain fought for the cause of the Spanish people.'

Ethel wrote these words later, when she was out of prison and far from Spain. In September 1937, when the article appeared, there were still international volunteers languishing in republican jails. Typically, Ethel made little of her own plight, which at one point looked grim in the extreme, preferring to talk about others and the wider problems in the country.

'Is it not ridiculous that a party of petty bourgeois and commercial elements − for that is what the Communist Party

175

in Spain consists of – should be permitted to destroy the struggle and all the efforts of the Spanish people? Stalinism, which has betrayed so many hopes of the workers in the past, must be arrested in Spain.'

As mentioned in the previous chapter, the PCE was much larger than the Communist Party of Great Britain, and drew its membership from a wider base. Here, though, Ethel focused only on the middle-class element, which was understandable given her experience in Catalonia where the vast majority of both industrial and agricultural workers were allied to the CNT. Anarchism in that region had captured the hearts and imaginations of the poor, while Catalan nationalism and communism drew more support from the middle class – an interesting subversion of the association of anarchism with bourgeois adventurism. Ethel had never visited Oviedo or Bilbao or Seville. PCE membership elsewhere in Spain, especially where industry was important, was made up of more working-class than middle-class people. Some may have argued that the Communist Party had *adopted* bourgeois policies and strategies, but the rank-and-file party member was less likely in those places to be a professional or involved in commerce, other than being on the factory floor or working the fields.

'The masters of Russia, fearful for their own future,' wrote Ethel, '. . . are using every method at their disposal to crush the workers of Spain. The actions of the Stalinists must be exposed to all the world. There must be continual protests at every Spanish Embassy . . .'

Not only communists, but many supporters of the Republic in the face of Franco's advancing army might have said that such a policy was suicidal. Creating international anti-Republican hysteria precisely at Spain's moment of crisis could only be self-defeating: the choice had to be between fascism and the Republic, as imperfect as the latter might be. But for Ethel, if there was no revolution, there was no war worth fighting. 'Anti-Fascism,' she would argue in October, 'is the new slogan by which the working class is being betrayed.'

No doubt Ethel voiced her views while she was cooped up with anarchist and POUM comrades. It is hard to imagine her dropping her voice as guards passed by; more likely, she argued directly with her jailers.

On 6 July 1937 Fenner Brockway was in Valencia meeting with government officials from the Foreign Office. He wanted to know what had happened to the British citizens who were prisoners in Barcelona.

Having promised Ethel that he would try and negotiate her release, Brockway was told in Valencia by the Spanish Foreign Office that there were only two British citizens being held captive in Barcelona. One who, it transpired, had travelled from Toronto and whose residence was there. And Ethel Macdonald. The case of the Toronto-based prisoner would presumably cause little difficulty for the British government, but Ethel was already causing too much.

Back in Britain tensions were on the rise, too. Harry Pollitt, General Secretary of the British Communist Party attacked not only the anarchists but the POUM and the – largely Scottish-based – ILP. David Murray, an ILP member from Motherwell, called Pollitt's remarks a 'gratuitous and venomous insult ... From Pollitt's nasty remarks one would almost think that there had been no POUM men in the trenches ... He said nothing of the members of the British Battalion who are hiding in the Spanish ports waiting to get out of the country. He forgot the group of men who are left to rot in jail in Valencia ...'

But there was tension even between pro-anarchist organisations like the USM and A-PCF, and Brockway and Murray's ILP. The latter had organised joint meetings with the London Bureau of the CNT. The USM felt that Brockway and his colleagues, not being anarchists, were merely making a public show of solidarity with the CNT for their own political ends. Emma Goldman became involved in the argument, but continued to work with the ILP. The USM, however, said publicly that it was having 'no truck with Brockway'.

The sectarian skirmish, however, did not prevent Fenner Brockway from representing Ethel Macdonald's case. On 8 July he returned to visit her in the Hotel Falcon. But Ethel was not there. Nor was the Toronto-based British citizen. The authorities had obviously thought it expeditious to have both prisoners released before Fenner Brockway's return. In essence, his negotiations in Valencia had worked – Ethel was free.

This news was in print in Britain by 14 July. According to the *Evening Times*, Ethel Macdonald apparently 'had accepted her arrest and imprisonment very philosophically'. However, although she was free, there appeared to be a problem. 'She is undecided whether she should come back to this country or stay in Spain ... It is Mr. Brockway's view that she would be wise to return home.'

The situation was not quite so simple. Had she left with Brockway himself she might have got away. But Brockway had other business to attend to – and so did Ethel. She had begun so many schemes, escapes and protests in prison that she could not simply walk away from them and let people down. She had friends and comrades to visit, people to thank and business to conduct with the CNT. There was also the matter of her personal belongings.

In various articles in the *Evening Times* and the *Sunday Mail*, she explained what happened after she left prison. 'I was released on visiting day. I shook hands all around and walked out of the door with the cheers of my comrades ringing in my ears. Outside, the Assault Guards congratulated me on my release!'

Once free, Ethel immediately made her way back to the centre of anarchist operations. 'At the CNT headquarters I was warned that the Guardias were still in possession of [my] house where I had been arrested, and that I would be re-arrested if I returned.'

Ethel went to the Council of Justice to reclaim her belongings that had been confiscated on the night of her arrest, including her passport and travelling papers. They, in turn, sent her and a recently released German volunteer to the police station on the Via Durruti. From there, she was referred, again, to the Council of Investigation in the Calle de Pavlov.

> Before we arrived, the German comrade warned me to be careful as it was the Spanish Cheka. I must say the atmosphere did suggest a place of torture.
>
> I was informed that under no conditions could I have my stuff, as it still had to be read and checked. I

protested and gave them a lecture on the conditions in Britain under capitalism and the conditions in the Spanish prisons, the treatment meted out to prisoners and discharged people in Spain. I was free. I was entitled to have everything of mine restored to me again. Then they got nasty and informed me that I was only at liberty provisionally, and that there was no doubt that, when they had gone through my stuff, I would be in prison again.

I got angry at *them,* and told them what I thought of them. They threatened to put me back in jail.

Of all the incidents Ethel describes – and she describes precious few involving herself – this one seems to capture her perfectly. Just out of jail, after negotiations at the highest level, and in the belly of the beast as she would see it, she lectured her erstwhile captors! This is the Ethel who lost her job in London for speaking out against management. Given the precarious situation she was in now, and her penury, Ethel wasn't arguing out of cupidity or dogmatism, but principle: a principle important enough to her to risk being sent back to the dreadful incarceration she had only that day been released from.

Then they accused me of reading the *Evening Times*. And of writing to you [the *Evening Times*' readers]. The paper had been sent regularly to me from the time I left Glasgow and I had clipped and dated a number of articles in its columns.

Also I had a copy of my letters on the Moscow killings and the question of Trotsky's asylum. All this had been noted by my questioners. In addition, they had seized a translation I had made on the subject of the Spanish imprisonments [written] by the Friends of Durruti.

'The *Evening Times*,' said the learned Russian Communist, 'is a Fascist paper, and you are a Fascist agent and ought to be shot.'

I told him not to be absurd.

The Russian wasn't the only one to accuse the *Evening Times* of being pro-Franco. The ILP's David Murray also believed the *Times*, and its competitor the *Evening Citizen* to be 'near fascist'.

However, the Durruti article was, according to the Russian, illegal. Ethel replied that she had translated it with the absolute intention of sending it abroad for widespread distribution. 'Because I believed in freedom, and neither Communists nor Fascists would suppress me.' She also told him that the *Evening Times* 'was an ordinary journal and was no more Fascist than the *Manchester Guardian*, and was more in sympathy, probably, with the Government than [she] was, since the Government, and not Franco, was recognised officially and diplomatically by the British Government.'

Still her questioners pressed. Her possession of an article delineating the situation of Republican prisoners and the fact that she had translated it, intending to circulate it, proved she 'was a Fascist beyond doubt'. Again, they threatened re-arrest.

More words were bandied back and forward and, in the end, they had no doubt as to what I thought of them and Russia . . .

Twice I had to go back. Each time I grew more and more certain that I was to be re-arrested. On the second occasion I was shown my possessions, and when I identified them I was told that I would be re-arrested once they had gone through [them].

In the end I got my passport and my money, but lost my papers and my clothes . . .

I am sure that the only reason I was not taken in right away was that I slipped out when I got a chance.

She concluded the telling of her story with a grim warning: 'Spain has been allowed to degenerate under the control of this Cheka directed by Moscow. Until the workers in all lands chase the CP and its connections from the earth, there will never again be a real working-class movement.'

Ethel was free from prison. But, without her papers, she was not free to leave the country.

In addition to her confiscated belongings, she had other possessions in her house, so one night she sneaked back there. 'I knew the place was still in the hands of the police and that I would be arrested if I was found there, but I waited until the caretaker had retired for the night and let myself in with duplicate keys of which the authorities knew nothing.' Ethel's dead-of-night adventure however, was in vain – her house had been stripped bare.

Now began a period of deep anxiety and insecurity in Ethel's life. Uncertain of her status, and of what she should do next, for the first time since leaving Glasgow, there was a sense of real distress in her narrative, and lack of resolve in her actions.

All this time I knew I was being watched. I never slept twice in the same place. One day, while I was sitting in a café, a man whose face was slightly familiar asked me if I was Ethel Macdonald. As I said Yes, I suddenly recognised him. He was one of the men who arrested me.

You can imagine my feelings. He then asked me if I went to that café every day. Of course I told him nothing, but after that I made doubly sure of my position at nights and when I was going about.

Believing that the safest place was nearest the enemy camp, I took a room right beside the Generalitat – the enemy's headquarters. As it turned out I was wise. They did not spot me there.

One day the British Consul found me in the street and hustled me to his office. There he told me that my friends in Britain and America were pressing for me to be sent home. I explained that I could not leave the country till I had a pass, and I could not get that till I had the pass to *stay* in the country. He said he would try to arrange things for me.

Either the consul had some difficulty in doing that, or he didn't try too hard – it would be some time yet before Ethel made it across the border. She explained the situation to Guy in a letter: 'I cannot get a visa. If I apply I shall be arrested. If I do not apply I shall be arrested. I can only leave the country with the help of comrades.

'I am quite well and am having thrills, but I do need your help and solidarity. Please do not fail me. I have had some terrible experiences . . .'

One of the 'thrills' was continuing to help others escape:

'I was surprised one day to find myself face to face with Bob Martin. He told me he had escaped from the prison. Watching his chance one rainy day he saw the guards disappear round the corner for shelter. He jumped off a balcony and raced in among the civilians who were hurrying to shelter. In this way he escaped, but the hue-and-cry was up in a very short time.'

Robert Conway Martin from Stevenston in Ayrshire had, like many volunteers from all over the world, begged and borrowed his way to France. There he embarked on the *Ciudad de Barcelona*, only to be jailed for his pro-anarchist views at Brigade HQ in Albacete. He escaped, and made his way to Catalonia, where he met up with more like-minded POUM militias.

Another stowaway, Alun Menai Williams, a Welshman, told the story in his book, *From the Rhondda to the Ebro*. Williams was a veteran of London's Cable Street Riot, and in May 1937, in France, was hoping to become a *brigadista*. 'I was on the *Ciudad de Barcelona*. There was quite a number of American volunteers in the ship.' There were also many Canadians – about 250 volunteers in all, including, it seems, Bob Martin from Stevenston in Scotland (and perhaps the Toronto-based captive Fenner Brockway had been told about). On 30 May the *Ciudad de Barcelona* was struck, and sunk, by an Italian submarine, only twenty miles from Barcelona, and two miles from the Catalan coast. Eighty men were drowned. 'It was in May,' Williams said, 'the water wasn't too cold, and I was a good swimmer.'

Many of the surviving volunteers were rounded up by Assault Guards the minute they hit dry land. Bob Martin ended up in the same prison as Ethel Macdonald.

Freed at last, he was in the same legal position as Ethel – without papers, and in fear of being arrested again at any moment. 'My job was to hide him,' Ethel wrote. They had made plans in the prison together, setting a place and time to meet should they ever both be free. On that day, Ethel had already scrounged clothes for him. She had looked for a boat to take him out of the country immediately, but had so far failed to find an amenable captain. 'For several days we hung about the dock . . . [though] I knew that the dock police would have been warned to look out for [him].'

Had Ethel been found helping an escaped prisoner her situation would have been made worse than ever. Her letters home during this period get gloomier by the day. In one, to Guy, thought to be dated 17 August (six weeks after her release), she wrote: 'You will have been expecting to hear from me sooner. Due to the usual – or unusual – unforeseen accidents, that was impossible.

'Most of the people I knew here left for their respective countries, and sometimes it is pretty lonely. My financial situation is bad.'

There were more reasons than ever before why Ethel was so isolated: moving from place to place meant that letters, or money sent out to her, could not be delivered even if they escaped the authorities' notice.

'From the clothes aspect, if I am not home soon, it will be too cold to be home at all.' The road between Barcelona and any of the border towns into France can become very quickly snowed up or iced over. Ethel and Jenny had travelled light to Spain and without suitable winter clothes. Moreover, Ethel had already given some of her clothes away to escapees.

'I am a terrible sight,' she wrote. 'I have lost everything. Don't worry. Perhaps you'll be seeing me soon. I guess you will. I hope so.'

While Ethel was living the life of a fugitive, the world beyond Spain was full of contradictory rumours about her. There were reports in English-language newspapers and in radical journals that she was still in prison, that she had been re-arrested, that she was being tortured, that she had escaped . . . 'You seemed to be under the impression that I had left Barcelona,' she wrote in another letter to Guy. 'But I am still here and unable to leave the country legally. First of all there is an order out for my arrest still, and there are seven charges against me. All very stupid but dangerous. Also, I am "in hiding" or living "illegally".'

Although Fenner Brockway had managed to negotiate Ethel's release from prison, he had not been successful in having the charges against her dropped, nor in ensuring her papers were organised so that she might leave the country.

'You must help. Not that I am afraid . . . But I would be foolish if I did not know the danger I am in now.' Letters between Guy Aldred and the ILP's David Murray, quoted in Daniel Gray's *Homage to Caledonia*, suggest that Ethel was re-imprisoned for two days in September – or at the very least, that Aldred believed she was. It doesn't seem unlikely, given Ethel's attitude to the Republican authorities. Murray was sceptical about the amount of danger Ethel was actually in. She had remained in Barcelona, Murray wrote to Guy, because 'she likes Spain and I think is in love with a fellow there'. If this is true, it is the only mention of a Spanish affair, but once again, it is unlikely that Ethel herself would never have written about anything so personal.

'It was Murray's feeling', writes Gray, 'that Aldred had allowed himself to be exploited by the press into validating anti-Republican stories surrounding Macdonald.' Aldred was incensed at the accusation. As far as he was aware, Ethel had been re-arrested and transferred to Valencia: 'I am able to say that Ethel Macdonald left Barcelona mysteriously and not of her own accord. Valencia is not the way to freedom, but to execution. Her situation is serious, most grave.'

According to Gray, Ethel spent a fortnight in a Valencia jail 'until finally Aldred was able to ascertain from the British Consulate in that city that she would be released in September before being transported to Nimes, in France, for urgent medical treatment'.

This is the second mention we have of Ethel being ill while in Spain, though she did not mention it herself either at the time or later.

The story of Ethel's final farewell to Spain, as she tells it herself, makes no mention of imprisonment in Valencia. Instead, it is after a prolonged period of assisting others to leave, finally only plucking up courage to do so herself by following one of her comrade's example. She took Bob Martin to the British consul – an official who, by this time, must have dreaded the appearance of 'the Scots Scarlet Pimpernel' and whomever she had in tow. He gave Martin a temporary passport. That document, however, still had to be signed by the police, who were hardly likely to help an escapee from one of their own jails. Ethel instructed Martin to shave off his beard and moustache. He had no choice other than to try getting his papers in order without being recognised.

It worked. A desk officer, faced with a long line of people with passports to be stamped, took Bob Martin's documents and, with barely a glance, stamped them all. The next day he sailed home on a British boat.

The ease with which Martin had got out of Spain persuaded Ethel that it was time she attempted the same. She had done everything she could for her fellow prisoners and escaping volunteers; she was running out of money, and perhaps her health was failing; her family, friends and colleagues were becoming ever more concerned for her safety and well-being. Yet Ethel wrote, some months after leaving Spain, that she was 'sorry to leave'. Difficult as her situation was Ethel Macdonald *wanted* to be in Spain. The greatest obstacle she had to overcome was her own sense of duty, and a feeling that this was the one great adventure of her life. She considered it a privilege to be in a country where a revolution first flourished and then came under attack. Leaving, for Ethel, was undoubtedly a kind of defeat.

'It was now my turn to get out of the country. I first went to get my pass to stay. The influence of the Consul secured it without much bother.' Doubtless he was only too pleased to be rid of her – he fined her a mere 25 pesetas for the favour. With the consul's authority behind her she converted the pass to stay into the more important pass to leave. The British official went with her to the docks, where, despite his presence, she was questioned again. 'But they allowed me to pass. I was never so thankful in my life.'

Still, she felt guilty at leaving behind so many comrades in prison and on the run, when she felt she could 'be of value both to them and of the cause'.

Ethel's family meanwhile had become convinced that she was dead. *Homage to Caledonia* quotes a letter they received from a Helen Lennox which must have dashed all their hopes:'The Secret Service operating today in Spain comes by night and its victims are never seen again. Bob Smillie they didn't dare to bump off openly, but he may have suffered more because of that. Your Ethel certainly believes his death was intended . . . What worries me more than anything is that Ethel has already been ill and would be easy prey for anyone trying to make her death appear natural.'

Ethel's mother fell back on her spiritualism, only to become convinced that she had lost her daughter forever. Daisy told the *Sunday Post* that she had heard the ghost of her dead child. 'As I have gone about my housework this week I have repeatedly fancied I heard a voice calling "Mother!"'

Andrew, for his part, remained in constant touch with the consul in Barcelona and the Foreign Office at home. He had written to Juan Negrin, the pro-communist prime minister of Spain. Negrin had replaced the more broad-church socialist Largo Caballero primarily because of the latter's mishandling of the May Day riots. Andrew's letter read:'Her [Ethel's] mother and I want her to come home . . . It is in your power to grant this request to grief-stricken parents. We are old folks, please relieve our anxiety.' The letter was published in the British press.

David Murray tried to reassure them in another letter: 'The friends and parents of Miss Macdonald may reasonably be anxious about her continued non-appearance. They should realise, however, that slow travelling and faulty postal, telegraphic and telephonic communication are normal in Spain.'

Andrew Macdonald's and Guy Aldred's supplications, and the pressure from Parliament and press had steeled the consulate's resolve to get Ethel out of Spain safely. Her parents must have rejoiced at a headline that appeared in the *Evening Times* as late as 24 September, saying that Ethel had left Spain.

Ethel was reported to have left the country on 4 September 'under escort' – presumably the consul – at least until she was safely aboard ship. She was now staying in Paris. The news travelled fast. The mainstream press in Britain and across Europe and, of course, in left-wing and radical newspapers and bulletins, celebrated the release of the Bellshill Anarchist (the *Daily Mail* getting quite the wrong end of the stick with the headline 'Scots girl freed by Franco'!). The organ of the French syndicalist movement, *L'Espagne Nouvelle*, devoted a full page to her arrest and imprisonment.

Ethel might have been out of Spain but her Spanish story was not quite over yet. She would not return to Glasgow until November. 'These were my adventures,' she wrote when she finally returned home and wrote up the story of her 11 months in Barcelona. 'They have been exciting and dangerous, but they were an experience which I would not have missed. For the sake of my beliefs, I would do the same again.'

# 10

# *The War to End War*

*∽ This struggle should have the assistance of all those who call themselves Socialists. But what do we find? There is no united action to assist the proletariat of Spain in their struggle. Instead we have a united front of Socialist and Communist parties with Capitalism! ∽*

Ethel's fame in the British press, the concern for her safety in Parliament and the public interest in her were something of a victory for an anarchist, a phenomenon never to be repeated since. Safely in France, there were requests from comrades she had worked alongside in Barcelona, as well as from political organisations and newspapers, to speak in all corners of that country. Her direct involvement with the Barcelona anarchists, her inside knowledge of Franco's recent advances, her political analysis and speaking skills, and the fate she had suffered at the hands of the Republic all made her a woman in demand. The French – their borders surrounded by the rising fascist states – Spain, Italy, Germany – were eager to hear what the Scottish revolutionary had to

191

say. For a few months, Ethel Macdonald became a leading light of the French left.

Ethel left no record of her escape from Spain, or her speaking 'tour'. We can gather, from remarks made in conversations and references in articles by herself and others over subsequent years that she sailed to France, probably to Marseille, and from there went to Nîmes. André Prudhommeaux – the French anarchist whose invitation a year earlier set Ethel's Spanish adventure in motion – organised venues for her under the banner of the rather wordily named Committee for the Aid and Succour of the Victims of the Counter-Revolution Communist Party Persecution in Spain. Nîmes was most likely where Ethel spoke first. After that, we know she spent some weeks in and around Paris, addressing political and public meetings.

Maup Stevens, the Dutch anarchist whom Ethel had helped escape Barcelona, then invited her to Amsterdam where she was given more platforms to speak of her experiences. The Dutch syndicalists also asked her to write a formal account of the persecution of anarchists in Spain.

None of the texts of these speeches and reports has survived – or, at least, no single article or manuscript can be accurately ascribed to that time in Ethel's life. But one complete article, published by the USM, is worth reproducing in full, as it provides a clear representation of Ethel's thoughts and attitudes around 1938. The title, 'The War to End War', above the badly typed leaflet, is scrawled in ink, in either Guy's or Ethel's own hand. The article is her assessment not only of the complexities of the Civil War but of contemporary Europe as a whole, and of the inevitability of a terrible confrontation with fascism.

The article is undated, but there are several clues in the first paragraph. The Chinese incident she refers to is most probably the Rape of Nanking, on 13 December 1937, or possibly the bombing of Chunking, both during the Sino-Japanese War. Part of Mussolini's tactical game with Hitler and the West was to pose as a 'peacemonger', and he called publicly for calm often enough in the years before World War II. Ethel is unlikely to be referring to as late as September 1938, when Il Duce spoke to the Munich Conference. As for Franco's preparations for an attack on Valencia and Barcelona, the Nationalists had been amassing troops and air power in the Balearic Islands since early 1937. During that time, those two seats of the Republican government had suffered a steady stream of bombardment, initially undertaken by the Italian air force and then the German Condor Legion, in planes launched from boats in the Mediterranean and, later, from the Nationalist-controlled Balearic Islands. In February and March 1938 the air raids intensified, destroying the harbour areas of La Barceloneta and the Ciutat Vella. Over 1,000 people were killed, making 2,500 fatalities since the beginning of the air campaign. As Ethel indicates that the Nationalists were *preparing* for a massive attack – which began on 16 March, her article must date from just before that; most likely between December 1937 and February 1938.

The Civil War at that time saw the crucial battle for Teruel in Aragon; the Republicans first took the city, only to lose it again to Franco six weeks later, on 22 February 1938. The Vatican, six months earlier in August 1937, had officially recognised the Franco regime – just a third of the way into the war, and only the third 'state' so to do after Germany and

Italy. This was unseemly haste, demonstrating how deep the divide was between Republicans and traditionalist Catholics.

It was an ever-darkening world for Ethel, beyond Spain's borders as much as within them. Hitler was making increasingly aggressive and open statements of his intentions for Czechoslovakia. The Nazi regime declared 'Gypsies' to be 'asocial', and Romanies were immediately rounded up and sent to concentration camps. In March, the German army entered and annexed Austria in the Anschluss. Prime Minister Chamberlain was trying to throw pieces of Africa to the Führer, hoping to appease him with new colonies. The failure of that policy resulted in Chamberlain's resignation in February 1938. The previous December, Nazism won power in Romania, and Italy had withdrawn from the League of Nations.

For Ethel, the battle was being lost on all fronts – ideologically, militarily, morally. And the lesson from Spain was not being learned. With the Communist Party ever more powerful within the Spanish Republic, radicals like Ethel pointed to events in the Soviet Union as proof of where Stalinism could only lead. In March 1938 the Trial of the Twenty-One – the final show trials against both the right and Trotskyists – was beginning. Repression of kulaks (landowning peasants) and ethnic minorities was at its height. Ethel's impassioned 'The War To End War' is a *cri de coeur*.

## The War to End War

What a mad world this is: A Chinese town of 500,000 souls destroyed in one swoop; more troops and war material being massed in the Balearic Islands for the attack on Valencia and Barcelona; within Spain itself, the reaction becoming more and more entrenched; and as the crowning point of this chaos, we have Mussolini's statement on the possibilities of maintaining 'world peace'.

There is no peace to be maintained. Today we are at war. Mussolini's proposals are but the throwing down of the gauntlet to Britain and France. In essence he says, 'Either Germany and Italy must be allowed to do as they wish, or we will oppose you.' And this is really what is desired – opposition in order to drown the world in another blood-bath, so that capitalism will survive still yet a few more years. Both Germany and Italy, as capitalist nations, are doomed unless they have war.

Fascism is military dictatorship. This necessitates huge standing armies provided for at the expense of the working class and the middle class. They must be provided with positions and salaries. The state cannot give these unless it expands. Expansion demands colonies. But unfortunately the non-independent countries of the world are already colonized. Italy and Germany are hemmed in. But expand they must inevitably, and thus war is thrust upon them.

Italy cast her eyes on Abyssinia. The troops of Mussolini murdered the people of Abyssinia by their thousands. But Mussolini did not gain from Abyssinia that which he expected. For many reasons – the climate, the mountainous country and the unconquerable spirit of the tribes – Abyssinia has been far too expensive to Italy. And so Italy must go elsewhere.

Germany, caught in a grip of steel owing to the conditions imposed upon her after the war of 1914–18, is in an even worse predicament. Her main industry since the rise of Hitler has been armament production. And no matter how useful armaments may be at a given time, unless there is a corresponding supply of food materials for the people her war material is useless. She too must have colonies.

The Mediterranean is the gateway to the rich colonies. The Mediterranean is controlled by Britain and France. Spain also holds a dominating position there. And so greedy eyes were thrown on Spain. There can be no doubt that the military insurrection by Franco was conceived and planned by Germany and Italy. In order to commence on their quest for colonies, it was necessary to have a military base in the Mediterranean. That they also expected Franco's 'Putsch' to be immediately successful cannot be doubted. Had Franco taken Spain in those first July days, the parts played by Mussolini and Hitler would not have been revealed. The alliance of Italy and Germany and Spain could have been superficially 'honourable'. But alas! The best laid schemes go astray. These Fascist leaders under-estimated the strength of the Spanish People. The workers in Spain rose, not only to rout their army generals but also to defeat the system that made such acts of treason possible. The plans of Hitler, Mussolini and Franco with reference to Spain opened up the way for social revolution.

As these plans were more and more frustrated by the indomitable spirit of the Spanish workers, Hitler's and Mussolini's assistance to Franco became more and more declared. German and Italian troops and war material were landed on Spanish soil, and Spain was subjected to the daily destruction of its towns and the callous murder of its people.

No longer could the intervention be concealed. But despite this, Britain and France not only refused to assist Spain, but under the cloak of non-intervention they aided Franco. Why? It must have been clear to the statesmen of these countries that their interests in the Mediterranean were at stake. And yet they permitted Germany and Italy to invade Spain. Why?

Had the Spanish people been supplied by other countries, as was their right, with war material, it is no exaggeration to state that the rebels would have been defeated within a very short time. But the victory of the Spanish people would not have meant a return to the *status quo*. Already the workers had seized control in Spain and were inaugurating a free society. Capitalism recognized the quality of the system that was being built in Spain. And this could not be tolerated. By helping Spain they would have cleared the path for their own destruction. But by helping Fascism they would not only destroy Socialism in Spain, but they could always deal with Germany and Italy at a later period. They knew that a Fascist Spain was but a step in the ambitions of Hitler and Mussolini. That the real goal of these gentlemen was the seizure of colonies in Africa, they understood. And would the workers respond to the call to defend the Empire? After the last war, this was very problematical. To cry 'Save Democracy' would have no meaning. There must be a slogan, a war-cry that would rouse the people willingly.

And so the farce of non-intervention was played. Spain was sacrificed for a slogan, 'Save us from Fascism!'

Now that the workers' cause in Spain has been liquidated, on the field of battle by Italy and Germany, and internally by Soviet Russia, the workers in other lands will be called upon to give their blood to 'save' it. Is not this logical? Will not the call go forth? 'Germany and Italy have gone too far. We must accept their challenge and save ourselves from Fascism.'

Hitler and Mussolini have been encouraged and abetted to the point that they are prepared to defy the imperialist world. Even they do not realize that they are but pawns in the hands of British imperialism.

'War to end Fascism!' Will the workers not respond? 'War to save Spain!' Unable to answer the call of the Spanish workers in 1936, they will rush to answer the call of a government when it is made. In this, the governments will be ably assisted by the Social Democrats, as in 1914, and also by the Communist Party. In fact, the Communist Party will be the chief recruiting sergeant for this war. 'Save Republican Spain! Save Soviet Russia! End the menace of Fascism!' And so imperialism will win again. So, for a time, will capitalism save itself.

Are we to go through another nightmare like that of 1914–18? Some may say, 'Let war come. After the war – revolution.' Well, I am not so sure. The last war gave us the Russian Revolution. Does present-day Russia make up for all the lives lost in that war? I say no! And must we wait for our governments to make the move? Are we not men and women with hearts and brains? Can we not decide our own destinies?

Not one life must be sacrificed to save capitalism. Capitalism must be destroyed, and we, if we but will, can destroy it without one unnecessary drop of blood being spilt.

War will not save Spain. War will not help the workers in Russia. War will not save us from Fascism; indeed, war will drive us to Fascism.

Today, Spain is lost. Today, Fascism under the cloak of Communism in Russia is strangling the cause of the proletariat throughout the world. Today, Fascism in Germany and Italy is menacing progress.

But Spain can be regained. Communism can once more triumph in Russia, Hitler and Mussolini can be swept aside for ever. Yes, all this can be done. This can be done by world social revolution – by the workers in Britain, in France and in all other 'democratic' countries bringing about the revolution at home.

Governments will never save the people. They exist to exploit and destroy the people. There is but one force that can save the people, and that is the people themselves. There is but one way of doing it, and that way is social revolution.

That, and that only, is the way to salvation.

~

Ethel returned home to Glasgow on 7 November 1937. She tried to do so quietly, but word got out; 300 people came to welcome her home. Doubtlessly Guy and Jenny and Caldy had failed to keep the secret. Even the press found out. The *Evening Citizen* reported that there was sadness in Ethel Macdonald's face the day she arrived home to Glasgow. 'I went to Spain full of hopes and dreams,' they reported her saying. 'It promised to be Utopia realised. I return full of sadness, dulled by the tragedy I have seen.'

Then she turned away from the reporters, but was heard whispering to Guy, Jenny and Caldy, 'It's terribly embarrassing. Please, take me away.'

Ethel had not suddenly discovered an aversion to public speaking – at least not yet – nor of having her words reported in newspapers. Simply, on this occasion she herself was the story and she always felt uncomfortable with that. Within weeks, as soon as she had visited her family and re-installed herself at 23 Gibson Street, she was off on a British-wide tour, speaking her mind at meetings and rallies in halls, on street corners and at Hyde Park about the British government being an accessory to the crimes that had befallen the Spanish Republic. According to Guy, she was invited back to France and 'associated with the Anarchist propaganda there'.

She began, and finished, the one and only speaking tour of her life in Glasgow's McLellan Galleries. One of her speeches, John Taylor Caldwell remembers, was called 'Spain – A Lost Horizon'. She told the story again of the communist attack on the anarchists, causing uproar in the room. 'There were several ejections. The uninitiated were confused. They did not know that, if the ghost of Marx haunted Central Europe, Bakunin and Proudhon had their own domain in the south of the Continent, and the old authoritarian spirit was still afraid of them.'

As Ethel spoke, through the last days of 1937 and into 1938, she watched, from a distance now, the slow, certain fate of Spain and its Republic. She read about it, saw the newsreels in cinemas, and – only a listener now – sat by radio sets as the Nationalist army advanced on Barcelona and

Madrid. Mussolini and Hitler formed the Anti-Comintern Pact a few days after Ethel's homecoming. The Axis was cemented: now the two forces she feared most were heading for inevitable war, while Britain still played at appeasement.

The final fall of Teruel came in February 1938 – incidentally the same month in which, as part of an *Evening Times* piece entitled 'Chance Changed These Readers' Lives', Ethel noted that meeting Guy Aldred was the moment that determined her future: 'As a working woman with no ambition beyond my class, it seems to me that chance certainly changed my life.'

The Italian air force began renewed and intense bombing on Barcelona the following month. In September of that year, the International Brigades were withdrawn and soon all foreign troops and volunteers were stood down. All the hope and optimism Ethel had felt for an internationalist uprising were in ruins. In November 1938 there was a last march in honour of the *brigadistas* in Barcelona. Missing were the many thousands who had lost their lives over the previous two years, including a third of the Scots volunteers. Ethel would not have wanted to witness that: a demonstration of defeat.

She would have read and heard about the Republic's trials of the POUM leadership. And, worst of all, Barcelona captured by Franco at the start of 1939. Madrid now, too, was doomed. The Republic tried to negotiate peace before the destruction of the capital, but Franco demanded outright victory. 'I'm prepared to kill half of Spain,' he said, 'in order to save Spain.' On 28 March, his victorious forces took Madrid. The Spanish Civil War had been lost.

From Ethel's perspective, however, there was one last twist. Before the final confrontation with the Nationalist army, a split opened up in the Republican government. Prime Minister Juan Negrin, together with the Communist Party, vowed to fight to the bitter end, believing there was still some hope of holding out against Franco. The chief of the Republican army in Madrid at the end of the war was Segismundo Casado, a soldier who had been key in organising the International Brigades. He had led at the Aragon front, and at the Battle of Brunete. Casado urged for more negotiation with Franco. On 5 March he ordered the arrest of communist officers. Two days later, Prime Minister Negrin and his Russian advisors left Madrid. On 8 March, fighting broke out between communists and followers of Casado. This time, the communists lost. Casado failed in his negotiations; Franco continued to demand unconditional surrender.

Over the next three years, the Nationalist regime killed over 200,000 people in reprisals, irrespective of the banners they had fought under. Socialists, Catalan and Basque nationalists, communists and anarchists were sought out and executed alike.

But as the war ended, and Falangist vengeance was wreaked, Ethel remained dynamic in her lectures: 'The Germans camped outside Madrid. The Italians camped outside Madrid. German planes, Italian planes bombed the city. And still Madrid held out. Durruti died. And still Madrid remained firm and Catalonia rebuilt the world.

'This was the Spanish revolution – challenged into existence by insolent Fascism. The workers of Spain rising to destroy Hitler, Mussolini and Franco.'

# 11

## Auld Claes and Porridge

*∼ Capitalists. Communists. No matter how they try to suppress us, the people will run out of patience with them! ∼*

Precisely one year had passed since Ethel Macdonald had left Glasgow for Spain. In that time she had seen the last glory days of history's only anarchist revolution and state. A world had ended, one war had been effectively lost, and another, global, battle darkened the horizon. Back in her old city, nothing had changed. Guy, Jenny and Caldy still worked out of the same office, furiously churning out pamphlets and newsletters, organising and attending meetings, making meagre meals for comrades at weekend confabulations. In Bellshill, Ethel's family were much as she had left them. Bessie was married, Carrie, the youngest, more settled.

Ethel was soon out again in the evenings and mornings selling her newspapers, back on the beat of 'the prosaic struggle of the everyday movement', as Guy Aldred put it. The streets hadn't changed: in George Square, office workers still rushed to tea-rooms for lunch; workmen and shop girls ate their pieces on benches in the square, regardless of the weather. Cigarette factory employees and tram and train workers changed shift according to the same patterns. Glasgow had as many poor as it ever had. The atmosphere was palpably different, however. Before her Barcelona adventure, when there was talk of war, it was Spain's war. Now the war everyone was discussing was one that would reach much closer to home. In 1936, galvanising the latent might of the working class to save Spain was hard enough; warning them now of the clash to come, in which, as Ethel saw it, the working classes would once again be cannon fodder for three different versions of capitalism, was almost impossible, but this was not going to stop her from trying.

In 1938 Jewish children first arrived in Glasgow, fleeing Nazi Germany and Austria. They were housed in Jewish homes in the city. Jewish traders boycotted German goods. In the same year, returned volunteers from the International Brigades, supported by a huge crowd of sympathisers, packed the City Hall in memory of 500 of their comrades who had already died in Spain. In the East End, the Norman Conks and the Shanley Boys, wielding knives and hatchets, fought a pitched battle in the streets. The minister of Glasgow Cathedral demanded that Kelvingrove Park be closed 'in the interests of propriety'. The IRA was suspected when 51 sticks of gelignite were found in a public toilet in Anderston Quay. Glaswegian refugees arrived at their 'safe houses' with only the clothes they stood up in. Glasgow was still Glasgow, in all its rage and poverty and drama.

~

Not long after Ethel returned, a letter arrived at the USM's offices in Queen Street. Sir Walter Strickland asked Guy Aldred if he would publish an anti-war article he had written, pleading with thinking men and women 'to stop this march of homicide'. Strickland, in the same letter, said he intended visiting Glasgow, ending his self-exile from the United Kingdom after 50 uninterrupted years. 'With Aldred's help,' John Taylor Caldwell wrote in *Come Dungeons Dark*, 'Strickland would launch a peace campaign, using his wealth (which was considerable) to bring influential world figures together.'

Walter Strickland and Guy Aldred's association spanned nearly 30 years. Back in 1911, when Guy had been imprisoned for publishing the article by Krishnavarma, Strickland had sent a telegram in support, declaring that Aldred had given him faith again in 'freedom-loving Englishmen'. He had also sent a donation of £10. Due to Strickland's avowal never to set foot in his home country again, the two men only ever met once in person; that was in the following year, 1912, in France.

Strickland was the son of a landed English family. He hated his aristocratic life so much that, in the 1890s, he left home, and England, forever. 'His estate was entailed,' Caldwell wrote, 'but when Walter inherited his father's money, he withdrew it from Britain and invested it abroad, from Brazil to Japan.' He spent many years in Java, India and Prague. 'Much of his energy was expended in denouncing imperialism and the White Man's Overlordship.' He became friends with many nationalist leaders, including Krishnavarma. Over the years, Strickland sent monies in support of Aldred's USM, but because he had repudiated British citizenship and had wealth invested abroad, it was often difficult for Guy to claim the contributions.

Their meeting in France was arranged to coincide with Krishnavarma's presence in Paris. There, Strickland suggested to Guy that he travel with him as a kind of companion-secretary. Aldred, however, was not a man to be anyone's second. 'It was not always a smooth friendship,' Caldwell says. 'Both men had minds of their own, and never trimmed a sail to catch the other's breeze.'

On his death in 1938, Strickland left his money for 'the furtherance of Peace', and Guy was appointed executor. Given the legal difficulties, only a fraction of the fortune was ever released – just about enough for the USM to buy some second-hand printing presses, and move their offices from Queen Street. The old premises were to be cleared for the upgrading of the Technical College into Strathclyde University. It was Ethel who found the Quartet's new working home, just around the corner at 104–106 George Street. They named the ground-floor office and shop space the Strickland Press, after their benefactor. No wages were ever paid. They worked 12 hours a day, from 9 a.m. to 9 p.m.

In February 1939, Ethel's suspicion of the Western democratic states' intentions for Spain were vindicated. Franco did not pronounce himself 'Caudillo', Generalisimo of Spain, until Madrid was secured by his forces on 28 March. A full month earlier, before the Nationalists had even begun their campaign on the capital, while Prime Minister Negrin and Segismundo Casado were debating over negotiations with the fascists, France, Holland and the UK officially recognised the Franco regime. To everyone who had cherished and defended the Republic, this confirmed the West's preference for a fascist, rather than revolutionary or communist, Spain. The United States waited until there was no option, recognising the regime in April. On the same day, Pope Pius XII enthusiastically welcomed Franco's victory.

Later that April, the British parliament, gearing up for war with Germany, passed the Military Training Act. Caldy remembers Ethel receiving her call-up papers for the women's National Service. 'She took out her blue marker and wrote "Get Lost" on it. After a few weeks, more papers arrived. She wrote "Come and get me". They never did. They must have heard about the notorious Scots Scarlet Pimpernel and didn't want her mounting escapes from a women's prison or something!'

Her decision not to fight against Nazism, however, will raise eyebrows. On the one hand, it is in keeping with a tradition of pacifist anarchism. Aldred had been a conscientious objector in World War I, and was imprisoned for it. Then again, both he and Ethel were fervent supporters of the war against Franco. Ethel would say that the opportunity to face and defeat fascism had been in Spain, where there was a genuine people's army opposed to capitalist oppression in all its forms. As far as she was concerned, the fight between the Axis and the Allies was between oppressors. The loss of 23 million Russians, for instance, and half a million Britons, was cause for mourning amongst anarchists; for communists and democrats, it was also the terrible price that had to be paid in the final defeat of fascism.

Once they had relocated to the Strickland Press, Ethel,

according to Caldy, laid down 'a firm dictum' that, unlike in Bakunin House, there would be 'no open house, and no welcome to gossips and idlers'. Despite Caldwell and Ethel being flatmates, comrades and occasional lovers, he is often curiously phlegmatic, even carping about her. It is hard to imagine bustling, talkative Ethel Macdonald laying down such a rule, let alone sticking to it. Her politics were forever evolving, most often through discussion and argument with others. But perhaps Caldwell has given us a significant insight into the woman entering her forties.

There were to be no more escapades like Barcelona for Ethel. In fact, as far as we know, she barely left Glasgow again, except to visit her family now spread around Lanarkshire. Perhaps she decided that her One Big Adventure had come and gone. Maybe she even felt some guilt at the failure of the Spanish Republic and the anarchist revolution. For the next 20 years, Ethel would work constantly and devotedly at the Strickland Press, but behind the scenes. She may have continued writing, but it is hard to differentiate between her words, Guy's, Jenny's and any number of colleagues. The old titles like *Barcelona Bulletin* and *Regeneración* gradually vanished. In their place came *The Word,* a frequently published, if irregular, publication of varying size and length. Ethel's name seldom appeared as a contributor.

In the spring 1990 issue of *Revolutionary History,* in a response to a review of *Come Dungeons Dark* in which Sheila Lehr complained that neither Jenny Patrick nor Ethel Macdonald 'come alive' in his book, Caldwell was uncompromising. 'Jenny and Ethel were not public figures. They worked in the Press, they did not write, speak or show any initiative in directions apart from printing at the Press, and attending United Socialist Movement meetings.' Lehr felt that *Come Dungeons Dark* depicts the two female members of the Movement as 'serving Guy politically', and as his 'appendages'. Caldwell retorted that the accusation smacked of male chauvinism. 'We did not serve Aldred. We served our political convictions. It was a case of from each according to his abilities . . . Guy was the editor and speaker: nobody else could or wanted to do that job. Ethel worked the press and did the books. Nobody else . . . Jenny hand-set and imposed the pages, and did the catering. Nobody else . . . I printed, guillotined, stitched, humped around the bales of paper, carted to the Post Office. Nobody else . . .'

This seems true of the period after 1938 up until Ethel's untimely death. The problem is that, in this letter, Caldwell is speaking of the group's entire life together, including Ethel's trip to Barcelona and before. Why Caldwell would want to say that Ethel was not a public figure and that she never wrote is puzzling; it is patently untrue. Doubtlessly, many of the articles that appeared pre-1938 under Ethel's name might have been edited and informed by Aldred. He may even have written whole sections. We could stretch a point to say that, even in her early articles from Spain, the hand of Guy was still present, with recent conversations, lectures, speeches still fresh in her mind. But her output of articles between November 1936 and August 1937 could only have been her own work. Also her own were her broadcasts, and the speeches she made in France and Holland before returning to Scotland. Jenny Patrick sent home copy from Barcelona and Madrid and wrote, quite independently of Guy, on behalf of the Anti-Parliamentary Communist Federation, long after he himself had stopped being a member. Lehr, it strikes me, has a valid complaint against Caldwell.

It can be argued, from the material accessible to us now, that Ethel, once she got into her stride after January 1937, actually *improved* as a writer, far from Aldred's influence. Her work during those six months is impassioned, personal, freed up from the minutiae and the ever-changing politics and re-positioning of Guy and the USM. Caldwell's claim is bizarre.

He was writing as an old man, more than 50 years after Ethel's one and only mission. The 23 years that followed were more fixed in his mind, a time in which it does seem that Ethel did little more than work the press and do the books. She had been to the front, risked her life, witnessed war and revolutionary struggle at first hand. Now she was resigned to working behind the lines. She never broadcast again. It must have disappointed Daisy, her mother, who had always seen a great career for her fifth child. As for Ethel herself, printing, collating, stapling, packing and distributing *The Word* was the great career she had always wanted.

Yet it is hard not to see that fate as some kind of defeat. Every movement needs its technicians and organisers and, by all accounts, Ethel fulfilled those requirements efficiently. But, knowing how she affected her readers and listeners, refusing to write can only be a withdrawal, a retreat.

A word on *The Word*, a strange title for a radical socialist-anarchist publication. Was Guy Aldred returning to his roots as a boy preacher? Caldwell thought there was a connection. 'Friends puzzled over [the name] and detractors sneered at it. It was chosen after much deliberation. The concept was not new in Guy's thought. It was present in his boy preacher sermons . . . To him it was the inexpressible element in man's unconsciousness that gave rise to change.' It was also, however, a jibe at Glasgow's City Fathers, a reference to the city's motto: 'Let Glasgow flourish by the preaching of the Word.'

Guy used the newssheet to republish many of the articles he had written over the course of half a century. 'The vote-catching politicians come and go,' he said, 'but I am always here!' He and the Quartet never took any holidays. On a Friday, however, they went to the pictures together – and during every film, Guy slept. Caldwell remembers him avidly recommending films to others later, and harshly criticising some, although he had snored through every one.

∽

The Spanish Civil War is to this day a faultline in the left. The failure of the Republic in the face of fascism is pondered, analysed and argued about. The central question is, who was to blame? Anarchists or communists?

In the 1960s, in *Revolutionaries*, Eric Hobsbawm wrote a scathing series of essays attacking the anarchists from a communist perspective, stating plainly that the failure was due to the anarchists, and criticising 'the remarkable ineffectiveness of the Spanish revolution'.

'Anarchism was a disaster,' he argued, 'because it made no attempt to change the style of primitive Spanish revolt . . . It legitimised the traditional impotence of the poor. It turned politics . . . into a form of moral gymnastics, a display of individual or collective devotion, self-sacrifice, heroism [and] self-improvement . . . It threw away political chances with a marvellously blind persistence . . . In brief, the main appeal of Anarchism was emotional and not intellectual . . . It is suitable that Spain, the country of Don Quixote, should have been their last fortress.'

Annie Murray, the Aberdeenshire communist, saw anarchy, not anarchism, in Spain. In *Voices from the Spanish Civil War*, she relates her experiences of anarchists in Barcelona when she was there in the summer of 1937:

> Oh, I knew the Anarchists! They would shoot anybody if they thought they were well off. Yes, they would just take them round the corner. You could hear the shots sometimes. They weren't very scientific in their approach, you know. We had them working in the hospitals and everything. They were a part of the International Brigade actually. But as I say they weren't very scientific in their approach to the whole cause. Nice enough blokes but they would shoot somebody if they thought they were well off – even just by the way they were dressed, you know.

Every critique of the anarchist left, at the time and since, pivots around those two notions – primitiveness and failure. Hobsbawm acknowledges the 'formidable intellect' of Noam Chomsky, and Chomsky answers Hobsbawm's points in his own series of essays, *The Responsibility of Intellectuals*. There, he talks of 'the failure of objectivity . . . of liberal [and Communist] intellectuals towards movements that are largely spontaneous.' They are regularly denounced as naïve, muddle-headed, and sentimental. If the Spanish Revolution is examined without prejudice, Chomsky claims, it will be seen to have been a 'remarkable success – until it was crushed by force'. He would also remind critics of the long preparatory period in which Spanish anarchism rooted itself, experimented, educated and developed its ideas.

Chomsky writes about the town of Membrilla in more depth in *The Responsibility of Intellectuals*. 'In its miserable huts lived the poor inhabitants of a poor province; eight thousand people . . .' But during the revolution, village life was collectivised. Chomsky quotes from a CNT study: 'Food, clothing, and tools were distributed equitably to the whole population. Money was abolished, all goods passed to the community, consumption was socialized . . . The whole population lived as in a large family . . . but it was under control because special privilege or corruption would not be tolerated.'

Chomsky suspects that such accounts only alienate anarchism's critics; they treat them with scorn, or interpret them as being in some way naïve or irrational. 'Only when such prejudice is abandoned will it be possible for historians to undertake a serious study of the popular movement that transformed Republican Spain in one of the most remarkable social revolutions that history records.'

Whether or not the revolution was genuinely successful, albeit for a short time, anarchism's enemies will proclaim that the greater good, between 1936 and 1939, was to defeat fascism. It has become a truism to many on the left that anarchists played at revolutions while Spain burned. The events of May 1937, it is argued, were mosly about a reaction by radical anarchist minorities against their own leaders, who had been willing to collaborate with the Generalitat and the Republic. Ethel takes the opposite point of view: 'Without the Anarchists the war would have been lost for the workers. And it is because of this that those who call themselves Socialists *refuse* to have anything to do with the Spanish Revolution . . . The Communists' opinion is that they demanded a firm and ruthless attitude towards those who, according to them, "sabotage the rear" . . . It was the activity of the Communist Party that brought about the May Days in Barcelona and worked for the overthrow of Caballero's government.'

David Murray, then a member of the ILP, was no anarchist but lauded the part they played in Spain: 'I myself greatly admire the Spanish anarchists, who are not the ruffians the papers here say, but are for the most part men of spirit and courage who have done most of the fighting. Today the Communist Party is going after them tooth and nail, as the anarchists want a real revolution and the Communist Party are only out for parliamentary democracy which is just what we have here. Imagine all that precious blood being spilt for nothing.'

Nearly 70 years on, the central criticism made of anarchism – that it could only lead to failure – looks different. Hobsbawm's contention, like the Communist Party's during the war itself, rests on the belief that only the hard realities of discipline and the sacrifice of some ideals will ever win out against capitalism, and that a period of dictatorship of the proletariat will be necessary to defend any victory until the State naturally withers away. But the communist revolution, we now know, was not ultimately successful. Seventy years of Leninism and Stalinism lead finally to defeat. So what, the Spanish anarchists would have asked, was the point in all that discipline?

Both sides accuse the other of playing into the right's hands. Some, in both sectarian camps, go further: the opposite side was secretly in league with conservatives and even fascists. There is no evidence for either accusation. Those who take the point of view that in 1937 there needed to be a single, regimented, resistance to Franco, feel that blaming the Communist Party for the May Days is part of a long history of anti-communism. Professor Willy Maley worries that it is political point-scoring to simply state it was 'those nasty Commies' fault'.

Willie continues: 'I think there was a lot of paranoia; conspiracy theories are unavoidable in war-time. When an opportunity for radical change presents itself, like it did in Spain, there will be differences and divisions. And they can only get deeper when that opportunity is lost. Isn't it unfair to all the courageous people, like Ethel herself, who fought, to ordinary men like my father, to dwell on the mistakes, blame retrospectively one party or another? To conjure up the spectre of Stalin, dismiss the communist effort and commitment in Spain as "spoiling the party"? That is simplistic. Sectarianism has riven the Left for a long time. It's a kind of ongoing McCarthyism.

'Before the Russian Revolution, anarchists were the West's great bogeymen – those unthinking, bomb-throwing malcontents. Since then and up until the fall of the Soviet Union and the appearance of the Islamic fundamentalist, communism was made to play that part. No anarchist was ever made to stand trial for anti-State activities in America. No doubt because it was communism that posed the greatest threat to capitalist domination.'

What is striking, however, is how little the divisions within the Republic seemed to matter, or even impact upon, the foot soldiers of the Spanish Civil War. Willy Maley has no memory of his father ever criticising the anarchists. 'It's more important to remember the sacrifice and courage shown by all who fought Franco. I mean there were anarchists who went to Eton, communists who went to Oxford and Cambridge, volunteers from the heart of Glasgow's East End. Anarchists like Ethel from Motherwell. There were different traditions and even within the Communist Party there were disagreements.'

Antonia Fontanillas in Dreux remembers the war and revolutionary Barcelona vividly, but cannot recall a single incident, argument, or even a conversation around sectarian divisions. In everything Ethel wrote, severely critical of the Communist Party, she utters not a word of criticism against the volunteers themselves, Spanish, Catalan, or international *brigadistas*.

The number of executions carried out by General Franco is estimated to be around 2 million. In a wholesale slaughter over such a long regime it is almost impossible to know the precise numbers of people imprisoned, tortured and killed. The 'Caudillo' openly set out to eradicate Spain of all his enemies: liberals, socialists, communists and anarchists. For several years after the war the country's prisons held hundreds of thousands of prisoners – even Himmler was shocked at the Spanish regime's enthusiasm for wiping out its political enemies. Between 1939 and 1943 alone, 200,000 people died at Franco's hands. The hierarchy of his beloved Catholic Church assisted him where they could, priests often reporting parishioners who had failed to attend mass before and during the Civil War, sending many of them to their deaths.

'Don't let me talk about that,' Antonia Fontanillas tells me, remembering the Nationalists entering Barcelona. 'I hate to think about it. I cried. I remember the Tuesday of that week. I was in the Workers' Solidarity office – I was working then as an administrator. A colleague, Hieres Nuñez, came in and said, "It's all lost. Whoever wants to escape there's a truck leaving this afternoon." When I got home that evening, I told my family, "Let's go". But my father wasn't well. He said he couldn't leave.'

A little later, stuck in Barcelona and hiding from Nationalist troops and policeman, Antonia went with her mother to the cinema. 'During the first days, when the Nationalists took over, my mother said outside the cinema, "If we go in we'll have to raise our arms in their salute. Otherwise they'll find us." "Me?" I said. "I'm not going to raise my arm!" We went in and there weren't many people there. When the moment came, my mother stood up to salute. I thought it was funny at first, and I stayed seated. A person behind me shouted, "You! You need to stand up." If I hadn't stood they would have put me in jail. It brought tears to my eyes.'

Catalan, Basque and all other 'minority' languages were proscribed. Regional-language street names were removed.

The CNT and UGT alike were outlawed, as were all political parties in any way opposed to the regime, including the PSOE, the PCE and the PSUC.

I first visited Spain in 1976, the year of Franco's death. The backwardness of a country after 36 years of dictatorship was astounding even to a teenager. Technologically, politically and socially the Franco regime left Spain in an unholy mess.

~

At the end of World War II, when the soldiers returned to civilian life, women who had kept industry and services going were unceremoniously dismissed. The Typographical Society, the Strickland Press's union, denied women the right to set type or to print. Ethel continued to work the machinery in contradiction of her union's rules. The Society, in reply, instructed suppliers to cease trading with Strickland for resisting the, clearly sexist, regulation. Together with the press's anti-commercial instincts – printing too many copies of their publications and charging too little – the Society's ban meant that Strickland teetered on the edge of bankruptcy.

And yet it flourished, albeit not financially. Throughout the 1950s and 1960s, Strickland was an important centre for anyone interested in politics and radical thought. Glasgow's present Lord Provost, Bob Winter, remembers the shop on George Street well. The headquarters of both the Labour Party and Communist Party, Colletts bookshop, the Clyde Press and Strickland, were all situated a short walk from each other between the City Chambers and the Saltmarket, forming a star-shaped hotbed of activism in Glasgow's heart. Bob Winter popped in regularly to all the bookshops, and remembers that Ethel was always at the Strickland Press. 'She was clearly the organiser, the person that kept the place running.' He saw Guy Aldred speak on several occasions, the 'Knickerbocker Rebel' fiery, compelling and unforgettable. 'Ethel Macdonald, on the other hand, seemed quiet. Polite and helpful, but definitely keeping behind the scenes. She struck me as an intense sort of person. Though not as intense as John Taylor Caldwell.'

Caldy described an average day at the Gibson Street flat. He always rose first, went for the morning rolls, made breakfast, and knocked on Ethel's door before he left for the press, where he lit the fires, swept the floor and got the machines ready. Aldred outlined a typical week: the entire Quartet working all day Monday to Friday. Saturdays, Ethel did the shopping, but still popped into the press to make sure everything was running smoothly. Ethel was living, in Aldred's words, a life of 'untiring active service in the cause, long hours of sometimes wearisome propaganda. She never gave up, though the rewards were very scanty, often not sufficient to keep body and soul together.'

She came home to Bellshill for regular visits, and Freddie Turrell remembers his aunt as being quiet, kindly, determined. On a few occasions in the mid 1950s, his mother Bessie took young Freddie to 23 Gibson Street. 'It was crammed full of books, newspapers, lots of copies of the USM's latest leaflets and posters.' Freddie remembers Aldred as a rather stern figure. 'Probably more to do with his hair being combed and waxed back in a severe way.' The front room was always full

219

of people, and loud with talk and discussion. Others who knew the place said there was always food, if cheap and hastily prepared for all comers. If Caldy's memory of Ethel's dictum that there would be no more open house as in the old days is correct, she failed to enforce it. Aldred, too, wrote about weekend evenings in Ethel's house, where they ate and discussed, and prepared lectures and speeches.

Freddie and May have many pictures of Ethel at the family home and on holiday with her younger sister, Carrie, on the Isle of Man. At this stage in her life, Ethel was closer than ever to her family. One of Freddie's keenest memories of Auntie Ethel was the day his sister Evelyn was born: 'I was at school and, when I came out at four o'clock, Ethel was at the gates to collect me. She told me the news, that I had a baby sister and said we should give my mum a wee rest. We wandered round for the rest of the afternoon. She took me to a café and bought me ice cream. We just chatted, about this and that. Nothing really. She was easy to talk to, a very calm woman. It was a really nice afternoon.'

A letter was published in *The Word* in 1960. R.M. Fox, who signed the letter, knew Ethel Macdonald. 'Characteristically,' Fox wrote, 'she told me very little about what she had done in Spain . . . She did not seek the limelight. It was enough that she had done what she felt to be right. No one could meet her without feeling the quiet purposefulness of her character.'

# 12

## *Stormy Petrel*

> ～ *Despite all the forces that stand in our way, working people of true heart and real bravery will continue to fight for Justice and Equality . . . The Revolution will one day happen! The low rumble of an eruption beginning deep down will eventually burst!* ～

In March 1959, Ethel took a tumble from a printing machine she was cleaning. She laughed the accident off and continued working, but in the weeks and months to come she suffered from continuous pains. Although Ethel seldom complained, it was obvious not only that the pain was intensifying, but also that the movement in her legs was becoming more and more restricted. Guy Aldred suggested she go to a doctor, but she refused. On May Day of that year Ethel produced a special edition of *The Word* and tramped all over Glasgow distributing it. When she returned to the press, Aldred had never seen her so exhausted. Finally, he convinced her to visit her GP, who diagnosed rheumatism.

Her condition became so bad that, according to Caldy, she was unable to board a tram. Rheumatism did not account for the rapidly increasing paralysis in both her legs. None of the Quartet owned a car – in Aldred's view such a possession was halfway towards class betrayal – so Ethel had to get around in taxis, a luxury the Strickland Press could not afford. Getting to and from her third-floor flat was a problem. Once again her friends pressed her to have a further examination and, on 13 October 1959, she was admitted to Knightswood Hospital. From there she was transferred to Killearn Hospital for further observation and treatment. She had walked into the ward in Knightswood but when she was discharged six weeks later she had to be ambulanced home and carried into her house. The consultant at Killearn had told her she must give up any hope of walking again, diagnosing a particularly virulent form of multiple sclerosis.

The four friends decided that she should move into Guy's flat in Baliol Street where he and Jenny could nurse her. Great strides had been made in the treatment of MS in the USSR and for months Guy tried desperately to import a vaccine from Russia. By the time it arrived, Ethel's condition had worsened considerably. However, when she started the course of 24 injections, Ethel brightened and became hopeful. Throughout her illness there was no lessening of her mental powers. 'I'm inside myself watching this happening to me,' she told Guy.

The serum did not work in Ethel's case, perhaps because the treatment was begun too late. The paralysis spread to both her arms. For a year, her friends nursed her attentively, during which time she said she knew she was dying. Guy tried to

222

secure another course of the Soviet injections, but she told him he was being foolish. The voice that had announced and explained the momentous events of Barcelona became slow and slurred. Eventually, with huge effort, she had to spell out each word she wanted to utter. 'Then her bright eyes softened,' Guy wrote. 'She smiled faintly, bravely. Very slowly she said: "I am sorry, Guy. Don't worry."'

By 1960 Ethel was completely paralysed and had to be constantly propped up in bed to prevent her tongue from falling back and choking her. 'Only her eyes were alive,' Caldy wrote, 'and only by these could she express her dreadful mental agony. She was still a woman of great power and vitality, imprisoned in a dead shell.'

Guy concurs: 'From the moment she fell from the machine till the time, 19 months later, when she made her last almost speechless utterance of despair, her mind remained strong and unimpaired. She never became adjusted to the slow physical death that gradually and relentlessly destroyed her.'

At nights she went to sleep sure that death was coming, and she awoke each morning with the feeling undiminished. Finally, in November 1960, she contracted pneumonia. She was taken back into hospital for oxygen treatment. She left the Baliol Street flat – a pivotal place in her life for nearly 30 years – with tears in her eyes.

At 6 a.m. on 1 December her friends were called to her bedside. The same call went out for Ethel's family a little later. Caldy remembered no acceptance or resignation in his friend's last agonised look at him and Guy. Unfortunately, Ethel's parents and her brothers and sisters arrived too late. Ethel Macdonald died at ten o'clock that morning in Knightswood hospital.

'I kissed her brow,' Guy wrote, 'and turned away in great sorrow.' She was only 51 years old; Guy was 74 and would live, very actively, for another three years. 'I felt that between the two of us I should have been the one who had gone.'

Aldred and Caldwell took a taxi back from the hospital. When they tried to pay the fare, the cabbie refused to take money from them as they were friends of 'the great Ethel Macdonald'. The news of her death had already been broadcast on the wireless.

~

Ethel's brief spell of fame in 1937 had returned when she became ill. For the last months of her life she had received letters and notes of support and sympathy. On her death, newspapers ran headlines to say that the 'Scots Scarlet Pimpernel' had died. In an extraordinary closing of the circle, for some reason the *Scottish Daily Mail* called her 'The Stormy Petrel of the Thirties'. The sub-editor on duty that day could not possibly have known that Stormy Petrel had been Andrew Macdonald's pet name for his daughter when she was no more than a toddler.

In another happy accident, decades later, an organisation Ethel knew nothing of, the Anarchist Communist Federation, launched a series of radical pamphlets, entitled 'Stormy Petrel'. Perhaps it was in honour of Ethel Macdonald, or perhaps, like Andrew, the Federation saw beauty and purpose in the rhythm of the seabird's flurry and float.

Aldred's obituary, in January 1961, is the most personal and distressed piece of writing he ever penned. His sadness at the loss of a friend and colleague is accompanied by a bitter, hopeless tone, evident nowhere else in over 60 years of articles, books and speeches. Guy laments that life generally appears to be without 'intelligence or aim . . . [there is] no generosity, no understanding'. Caldwell believed that Guy still had not recovered from the loss when he himself died. Although the remaining three of the Quartet worked on in the Strickland Press, after Ethel's death *The Word* had to be reduced in size and circulation. Debts rose and income fell away. The smell of damp pervaded the old building in George Street; the ancient machines began to suffer from rust and lack of care. But the trio worked on as best they could – Guy had made a promise in Ethel's obituary: 'to be bold in mind and spirit so as to play my part in bringing about the new world in which Ethel Macdonald believed'.

To the best of my knowledge there is no memorial to Ethel. Certainly, there is no grave. Guy Aldred wrote that Ethel had arranged to leave her remains to medical science.

Ethel Macdonald's life seems like the night sky, briefly lit by the comet of the Spanish Revolution, which allows us to glimpse the shape of things. But for Ethel, Barcelona was simply one element in a lifelong mission, no more important than standing for hours on street corners distributing leaflets, or keeping a printing press running for longer than it was designed to do. From the family and industrial politics of the Edwardian Steel Town, the women worn down by work and poverty, suffragettes in the headlines, to that last May Day of 1959 spreading *The Word*, Ethel's journey has logic and consistency. Each event and encounter in her life builds towards a trajectory: Daisy, that very 'Victorian' working-class mother who saw possibilities for her daughter; the unnamed American sailor, Ethel's only true love affair, ending in betrayal and the loss of her child, an experience that instead of embittering her drove her to tackle sexism and the power of Church and State; experiencing capitalism first-hand in London. She would have agreed with Noam Chomsky, who told me that, in a very important sense, fascism had won in the West. Corporations and companies are perfect models of totalitarian power: utterly hierarchical and dictatorial, the role of the capitalist state is merely to protect a conglomeration of authoritarian units under the guise of democracy. Ethel herself in fact stated, 'Fascism is not something new, some new force of evil opposed to society, but is only the old enemy, capitalism, under a new and fearful-sounding name.'

Not all who knew her would agree that her life and words help us see the shape of things. David Murray, of neighbouring Motherwell ILP, who reported on Bob Smillie's death and Ethel's own treatment by the Republic, found her little short of infuriating: 'She may have had disagreeable experiences but was never in any danger of being "bumped off". She also had ample opportunity to leave Spain, where she was performing no useful work for anybody. She entirely neglected to learn Spanish to any degree. Every little bleating message which came from Spain about her was given full publicity in the Glasgow *Evening Times*.'

It is safe to say that, as well as their political differences, Murray's and Macdonald's personalities clashed resoundingly. Anyone of Ethel's energies and opinions is bound to make enemies.

With Guy and Jenny and Caldy, on the other hand, she

was a kindred spirit. Together they lived and breathed and experimented with radical modern thought, reacting to the Russian Revolution and how it played through their generation. Not just thinking deeply about organisation and authority – Marx and Bakunin, internationalism, sexual politics, pacifism and revolution – but acting on their principles. It was the two women of the Quartet who came face to face with the enemy and the obstructions to freedom, and Ethel alone who suffered the consequences of idealism gone wrong. The final 23 years of her life were active and demanding, a forward thrust towards peace, justice and understanding; her illness was another human battle waged against impossible forces.

'She was somebody,' Willy Maley feels, 'who felt she could make a difference. A great example of female heroism that you see right throughout that period and certainly during the Spanish Civil War.'

Willie McDougall gave the tribute at the humanist ceremony after her death. He had been the leading light of the Anti-Parliamentary Communist Federation during the split with the United Socialist Movement before Ethel and Jenny went to Spain.

Ethel herself would have disliked the singling out of one person in a global struggle for a better world. Her relevance to us today is partly due to the company she kept and the people she worked with. The list reads like a roll-call of progressive spirits: Guy Aldred, Emma Goldman, Buenaventura Durruti, James Maxton, Bob Smillie, Jane Hamilton Patrick, Fenner Brockway, André Prudhommeaux, Augustin Souchy. And those to whom Ethel was connected by association: George Orwell, whose experiences in Barcelona matched Ethel's so closely; La Pasionaria, who took a radically different line, but whose background and dedication are echoed in Ethel's life; the pacifist Walter Strickland; Arthur Koestler; Antonia Fontanillas and all the other working-class women whose lives and hopes were suddenly – if briefly – transformed; the *brigadistas* from every country who went to fight in Spain and got caught up in a fundamental argument over the future.

Antonia Fontanillas finishes her interview with me on a hopeful and defiant note. The ideals she believed in as a teenager in revolutionary Barcelona she still sees today, in people 70 years younger than herself. 'No matter who it upsets, our truth will continue to be. Do not bury us; we are not dead yet and there are youth that will continue to fight for what we believe in,' she tells me.

~

May Day, 1959. Ethel has trudged all over Glasgow. From the Strickland Press through the Trongate, out east to Bridgeton, past the Grand Orange Lodge to Parkhead, a city on the move from single-ends and back green toilets to the gleaming new Easterhouse, and over the river, Castlemilk. She hustles the cinema queues waiting for *Some Like It Hot*, and a few people buy a copy of *The Word*.

Castro has ousted the Cuban dictator Batista, a new revolutionary government sits in Havana, full of promise and possibility. There's an election due in Britain. Ethel knows that the Tories under Harold Macmillan will win again, despite Gaitskell's lead in the polls, despite Suez, despite the British people being lectured that they'd 'never had it so good'. For Ethel it will make little difference: Labour would change nothing.

As she wends her way back to the shop, she slows down. This pain she feels is more than fatigue; it is the birth pang of a disease that, in just over a year, will paralyse, silence and eventually claim her. She's spent so much of her life walking – in the Highlands, with Lyons' clients in London, around these same Glasgow streets for 30 years, and of course, halfway to Barcelona and endlessly round the Raval, up and down the Ramblas. Birds winging freely over the Generalitat, those hopeful soldiers, women and men, in their Glengarry bonnets and red-and-black neckties – she can still see them in the faces around her now. Despite the poverty and defeats, she sees hope in tired eyes, determination in the youngsters running around, a decency she has known since childhood on Andrew's knee, at Daisy's side. Barcelona was only special because circumstances allowed ordinary people to seize power and, for a while, show what was possible.

We can be sure that as she does her daily rounds she thinks often of Jara and the Marías, exiled far from their beloved Sabadell, of the solid friends from all over the world she met in Catalonia – Sacha, Maup, the brave Germans and Italians. They're all here in Glasgow on the eve of a new decade. Those same spirits in the cinema queues, at the shops, at the turn-out for the May Day march in Glasgow Green; a yearly celebration when socialists, communists and anarchists march together, if not side by side. Marxists most of them, but still divided, their dreams frozen in the Cold War.

Barcelona is a state of mind now. But that thirst for freedom, for equality, is still there. It seized the day in Cuba; and will do so again, somewhere. Perhaps next time the way ahead will be less clouded. The springs of revolt against dehumanizing capitalism are many – they can be found in meeting rooms, Trades Union halls, churches and clubs, amongst the rank and file of many -isms. Ethel was never the negotiator, the finder of common cause. She was energy, dedication; a firm believer in humanity's possibilities. We need her kind too.

Her last May Day, 1960 – May days had always been dramatic. No less so as her body fails her but her mind battles on. Ethel Macdonald: small, neat, intense. She can't smoke any more, or even speak fluently. She must think that all in all it was an eventful life, one in which she tended her own garden, planting bright, red, flowers that will bloom long after the gardener has gone.

∽

'It's easy to forget that great events, great movements, consist of lots of ordinary people. The business of actually building a movement is done by people whose names we may never get to know,' Mike Gonzalez reflects. 'In this case we have got to know one of those names. And so I see Ethel as heroic in her way, courageous, but representative of a great movement. Her story is one of how individual private lives meet great historical events. In that sense Ethel Macdonald's life continues to be hugely significant for us, for the generations that followed.'

Ethel's, at times, stormy words and divisive thoughts reflected her experience of the world, split into pacifists and freedom fighters, parliamentarians and anti-parliamentarians, leaders and grassroots, nationalists and internationalists. She was an example of Caledonian, and radical, antisyzygy: progress needs big spirits and minds, capable of accommodating contradictions. The future lies, as Hugh MacDiarmid wrote, 'whaur extremes meet'.

In a turbulent world where ideas were tumbling over each other, from the very beginning, Camelia Ethel, the Scots Scarlet Pimpernel, the Stormy Petrel, had her eyes fixed calmly on one primary goal: freedom.

# Select Bibliography and Suggestions for Further Reading

*Note: The quotations at the start of each chapter are all Ethel Macdonald's words, and are taken from her articles, letters, diaries and essays. Many of these are part of the Ethel Macdonald Collection in Glasgow's Mitchell Library, which was an invaluable resource during the research and writing of this book.*

Bakunin, Mikhail, *Statism and Anarchy* (Cambridge University Press, 2007)

Buchanan, Tom, *The Impact of the Spanish Civil War on Britain: War, Loss and Memory* (Sussex Academic Press, 2007)

Caldwell, John Taylor, *Come Dungeons Dark* (Luath Press, 1988)

Chomsky, Noam, *The Chomsky Reader* (Pantheon, 1987)

Connolly, Cyril, 'The Anarchist Revolution in Spain', *New Statesman* (21 November 1936)

Fyrth, J. and Alexander, S., *Women's Voices from the Spanish Civil War* (Lawrence and Wishart, 2008)

Goldman, Emma, *My Disillusionment in Russia* (Williamson Press, 2007)

Gray, Daniel, *Homage to Caledonia; Scotland and the Spanish Civil War* (Luath Press, 2008)

Hobsbawm, Eric, *Revolutionaries* (Abacus, 2007)

Hodgart, Rhona, 'Ethel Macdonald: Glasgow Woman Anarchist' (Kate Sharpley Library, 2003)

van Holden, Oliver, *Old Motherwell and Newarthill* (Stenlake Publishing, 2000)

Ioannou, Gregory, *British Anarchism and the Spanish Civil War* (Νεκατωματα, 2003)   Available online at: nekatomata.blogspot.com/2006/11/british-anarchism-and-spanish-civil-war.html

Kenna, Rudolph and Sutherland, Ian, *They Belonged to Glasgow* (Neil Wilson, 2001)

Lennon, Peter, 'A Priest Was Firing at Us' (*The Guardian,* 10 November 2000)

Macdonald, Ethel, 'The Volunteer Ban' in McLay, Farquar (ed.), *Workers City: The Real Glasgow Stands Up* (Clydeside Press, 1988)

Murray, Annie, *Voices From the Spanish Civil War* (Spartacus Educational, 1986)

Orwell, George, *Homage to Catalonia* (Penguin, 1989)

Pitt, Bob, 'Land and Freedom: A Reply to Jeff Sawtell' (*What Next?*) Available online at: http://www.whatnextjournal.co.uk/Pages/History/Loach.html)

Prasad, Devi, *War is a Crime against Humanity: The Story of War Resisters' International* (War Resisters' International: London, 2005)

Robert, Kern, 'Anarchist Principles and Spanish Reality: Emma Goldman as a participant in the Spanish Civil War', *Journal of Contemporary History* (vol. 11, no. 2, July 1976) pp. 237–259

Souchy, Augustin, 'The Tragic Week in May' in Souchy, Augustin; Peirats, Jose; Bolloten, Burnett; Goldman, Emma, *The May Days: Barcelona 1937* (Freedom Press, 1987) pp. 30–1

Williams, Alun Menai, *From the Rhondda to the Ebro: The Story of a Young Life* (Warren & Pell Publishing, 2004)

'Anarchism in Glasgow: Charlie Baird Snr, Mollie Baird, John Taylor Caldwell, Babs Raeside' (transcription of a public discussion that took place August 1987; available online at www.raforum.info/article.php3?id_article=3588)

# *Acknowledgments*

My thanks for all the excellent work done, and the assistance given to me by Rhona Hodgart, Alison Murphy, Freddie and May Turrell, Antonia Fontanillas, Mike Gonzalez, Mark Littlewood, Willy Maley and Daniel Gray.

Thank you, Noam. (Writing the book was worth it just to say that.)

Too many books, essays, pamphlets, internet articles, letters and transcripts to mention were read over four years of working on *An Anarchist's Story*, film and book. I have tried to cite them whenever necessary or possible. Andy Durgan, Eric Hobsbawm, Charlie Baird, Farquar McLay, George Orwell, Tom Buchanan, Anthony Beevor, Paul Preston, Hugh Thomas, Gerald Brennan, Gabriel Jackson, Rudolph Kenna and Ian Sutherland, Andy Walker and John Simkin, Rhona, Alison and Daniel again . . . I can name but a few. Together, alongside conversations and interviews, they make up the volume you have in your hands.

For the invented conversations and scenarios that pepper this biography, I take the sole blame.

To Hugh Andrew, Peter Burns, Andrew Simmons and Kenny Redpath at Birlinn, for their support, patience and advice. The honourable art of editing is still alive and robust in Sarah Ream's hands. Thanks.

Geraldine Cooke, for even more patience and advice. The staff of the Mitchell Library, for humphing great boxes of papers out for me on a regular basis over the writing of the book. Mike Gonzalez again for reading early versions, and for advice that dates back further than either of us will admit.

They might be surprised, but shouldn't be – Rosemary Goring, Bruce Young, Eric Coulter, Ana Zabalegui, Judy Moir, Leslie Finlay, Carolyn Beckett, Jean-Louis Rodrigue, David McLennan and Les Wilson, for their friendship, encouragement, and keeping bread on our table.

And the most important thanks of all to Moira, Emma and Daniel. *Basta ya.*

# Index

*Note: In a few entries 'EM' is used to stand for Ethel Macdonald*